THE
SHAAR
PRESS

THE JUDAICA IMPRINT
FOR THOUGHTFUL PEOPLE

TWERSKI

ON

A SHAAR
PRESS
PUBLICATION

SPIRIT-UALITY

RABBI ABRAHAM J. TWERSKI, M.D.

Published by **SHAAR PRESS**
Distributed by MESORAH PUBLICATIONS, LTD.
4401 Second Avenue / Brooklyn, N.Y 11232 / (718) 921-9000 / www.artscroll.com

Distributed in Israel by SIFRIATI / A. GITLER
6 Hayarkon Street / Bnei Brak 51127

Distributed in Europe by LEHMANNS
Unit E, Viking Business Park / Rolling Mill Road / Jarow, Tyne and Wear / England NE32 3DP

Distributed in Australia and New Zealand by GOLDS WORLDS OF JUDAICA
3-13 William Street / Balaclava 3183, Victoria, Australia

Distributed in South Africa by KOLLEL BOOKSHOP
Ivy Common / 105 William Road / Norwood 2196, Johannesburg, South Africa

ISBN: 1-57819-257-9 Hard Cover
ISBN: 1-57819-258-7 Paperback

Printed in the United States of America by Noble Book Press
Custom bound by Sefercraft, Inc. / 4401 Second Avenue / Brooklyn N.Y. 11232

Table of Contents

Introduction

here has recently been a great increase of interest in spirituality. There are generally reasons why a certain phenomenon occurs at a particular time in history, and the reason for the upsurge of interest in spirituality is not difficult to determine.

Until relatively recently in history, life was a difficult ordeal. As late as the turn of this century, epidemics decimated entire communities, childhood diseases claimed the lives of many children, new mothers died in childbirth, infant mortality was high, and tuberculosis truncated many young lives. The average life span was under 40. Work conditions were strenuous, with many hours of hard physical labor required to earn one's livelihood. Travel was time consuming and arduous, and communications were fraught with lengthy delays. Climatic conditions were often virtually intolerable, and although one might warm up with a pot-belly stove or at the fireplace, there was no escape from torrid heat.

The genius of science and technology in this century has been spectacular. Immunization has eliminated epidemics and many childhood diseases. Antibiotics have cured the lethal childbed fever, and there is not a single tuberculosis hospital in all America! Work conditions are quite comfortable, with much of the labor being done by machines, often controlled by electronic devices. Jet flight gives one access to remote lands within hours, and the telephone permits immediate contact around the globe. Microwaves reduce cooking time to minutes, and efficient furnaces and air-conditioning allow one to live in comfort, while entertainment is brought into the home via the media. Many of the miseries and distresses of just several decades ago have been eliminated by human genius.

Obviously, mankind is still unhappy. The incidence of alcoholism and drug addiction, especially among young people, indicates that all the comforts of modern living notwithstanding, mankind is nevertheless discontented. Psychiatrists and psychologists are not at a loss for patients who are dissatisfied with life. Let us therefore reflect: *What is there that human genius can do, either technologically or scientifically, that can make mankind happy?* While there is now hope that a cure for cancer will soon be found, will that great achievement really eliminate mankind's doldrums? I know that it is politically incorrect to say this, but let us realize that prolongation of life is not an unmixed blessing. There are now states that deny payment for certain medical procedures after 80, and the single greatest concern that occupies both the executive and legislative branches of government is what to do about the social security system and runaway Medicare costs. Let's face it. The cure for cancer will be hailed as a marvelous medical accomplishment, which it certainly will be, and many individuals will be most thankful for this medical breakthrough, but society as a whole will be hard pressed to support the care necessary for the ever-increasing population.

Insofar as technology is concerned, just what are we lacking that could give us happiness? Digital television? Computers with a more rapid download? Copiers that will duplicate more quickly? Perhaps you can think of something that I cannot.

I believe that we have come to realize that while science and technology have indeed provided greater comfort, and have made life much easier, *they have not and cannot give us a reason for life or an ultimate goal in life.*

The phenomenon of the 60s and its aftermath may be due to the reasoning that the unprecedented marvels resulting from man's genius have obviated the need for anything transcendental. Science and technology had so revolutionized life with their amazing feats, that they would no doubt soon solve *all* humans problems, hence the motto among the young visionaries that "G–d is dead." But alas! The next few decades demonstrated the limitations of science and technology, and people have come to realize that the search for happiness must be directed elsewhere, hence the interest in spirituality.

The drug epidemic on the one hand and the flight to cults on the other indicate the depth of dissatisfaction that prevails today. These desperate attempts at finding some comfort or purpose in life are by no means limited to people who feel disenfranchised and who despair of the opportunity to advance themselves. Drug use and cultism are prevalent among the affluent of society who lack for nothing. One cannot come to any conclusion other than that there is a disillusionment with the material world, and people are groping for anything that promises them relief from a feeling of futility, which results in the increased interest in spirituality.

Definition of Spirituality

Spirituality is a frequently used term, but one which is rather difficult to define; indeed, spirituality may mean different things to different people. What I am about to present is a definition which I have been using in my work. It is certainly not the final word on the subject.

Let me first state what Jewish spirituality is *not.* Spirituality is not withdrawing from society and isolating oneself as a recluse, eating the bare minimum to remain alive and sleeping on the ground, spending the entire day in prayer and meditation. During the time of the Second Temple there was a sect of Essenes who separated themselves from society to devote themselves totally to prayer and study of Torah. They rejected anything that provided physical gratification, and they therefore abstained from eating meat, drinking wine, and getting married.

This is not the type of spirituality the Torah advocates. We are permitted to eat meat and drink wine judiciously, and we are required to marry and have families. We should work and engage in commerce. In short, we are to lead normal lives, but all the activities of normal living should be within the scope of spirituality.

The Torah states, "You shall be holy people unto Me" (*Exodus* 22:30), and the Hebrew lends itself to the interpretation of Rabbi Mendel of Kotzk: "You shall be humanly holy." We are not expected to be angels. To the contrary, we are supposed to be human, but spiritually so.

A wealthy chassid once boasted to his Rebbe that he has a separate house where he resides only on Passover, and no chametz ever enters the house. In this way he is absolutely certain that he is in complete compliance with the Torah requirement to be free of all chametz on Passover.

The Rebbe was not at all impressed. "What you are doing is actually contrary to the wishes of the Torah. The point is precisely to have chametz all year round, and to dispose of it on Passover. Not having the need to search after chametz and clean the house thoroughly defeats the purpose."

What the Rebbe was referring to is the symbolism of *chametz* as representing the *yetzer hara*, the drive to gratify our physical impulses. We know we have a *yetzer hara*, and we must work diligently to rid ourselves of it. Not to have *chametz*, i.e., a *yetzer hara*, is to be an angel. We are to be holy humans, not angels.

Before tackling spirituality, let us try to define a more elementary term: *humanity*.

You may say that this is hardly necessary, since humanity has been adequately defined in science. In Biology 1 we learned that the human being is *Homo sapiens*, a classification which is universally accepted. If you were told that you are a *Homo sapiens*, you would in all likelihood say, "Yes, that is what I learned in high school." You would not be offended by this term.

Perhaps your acceptance of this appellation is because it is in Latin, hence it sounds rather sophisticated and quite innocent. But let us see what it means when translated into English. *Homo* refers to a genus, a family of animals of which man is a member, and he shares this genus with other hominoids, such as monkeys, gorillas, baboons, orangutans, chimpanzees, etc. Man is distinct from the other members of this group by being a species of *Homo* which is *sapiens*, a term which essentially refers to intellect. *Homo sapiens* thus means "a baboon (or ape) with intellect," and I am sure that none of us would find this term complimentary.

While intellect is an important and distinct trait of man, it is not the only feature which distinguishes him from animals. There are a number of other traits which are unique to man, and therefore, along with intellect, comprise the definition of man. Allow me to list several of these.

A human being has the capacity *to learn from the past*. Animals may indeed learn from previous experiences, such as to avoid things which were injurious to them, but they are certainly unable to learn from the experiences of past generations.

Suppose a race horse runs the Kentucky Derby and loses by just a neck. This horse sires a foal which grows to be a fine race horse, and eventually runs the Kentucky Derby. Learning from the past would mean that this second generation horse can study the race its father lost to discover where he had erred, and by avoiding this mistake this horse now wins the race. We will all agree that this is something which is not possible for any animal to do. Learning from the past is therefore a uniquely human trait, and is therefore part of the definition of man.

A second feature that is uniquely human is *the capacity to think about the goal and purpose of one's existence*. It is safe to assume that animals do not reflect on the purpose of their existence, and while some people may not do so either, they nevertheless have the *ability* to do so, an ability which animals lack. Even if one does not arrive at any conclusion about the purpose of one's existence, the very capacity to give this thought is unique to man.

One might perhaps challenge with, "How do you make such assumptions about animals? Perhaps they do have these capacities, but we are unaware of them." To this I respond, how do you know that animals are not

sapiens? Perhaps they have the equivalent of the dia-
logues of Plato of which we are unaware, just as they are
undoubtedly unaware of human knowledge. Inasmuch
as no one seems to challenge the scientific assumption
that intellect is unique to man, I assert the same right to
assume that animals do not have these other capacities
which are therefore uniquely human.

Let us continue. Man has *the capacity to volitionally
improve himself.* It is unlikely that a cow, for example,
ever thinks, "What must I do to become a better cow?"
Only a human being can reflect on and implement self-
improvement.

Animals are born essentially complete, and change
only by growing larger and stronger. There can be some
rather radical changes, such as when the lowly caterpillar becomes a beautiful butterfly. While this is certainly
an improvement, this is not something which the caterpillar decides to do volitionally. A caterpillar is certainly
not capable of saying, "I am afraid of heights, and I do
not wish to become a butterfly and be up in the air. I prefer to remain a caterpillar and remain safe on solid
ground." It is programmed into the caterpillar's genes
that at some point in its life cycle it will spin a cocoon
and emerge a butterfly, whether it wishes to or not.
Hence, even the caterpillar is born complete, and cannot make any *volitional* changes. This is something
which only a human being can do. Furthermore, regardless of one's genetic composition, a person can make
salutary changes in himself.

An animal does not have *the capacity to delay gratification.* Whatever an animal desires, it will attempt to

get. A human being may have a desire and the means to achieve it, but may postpone it to a more appropriate time. He may very much desire to embark on a scenic cruise to a beautiful place and he may have the money to do so, but he may decide to postpone it until he is free of certain obligations. This trait, too, is uniquely human.

A human being can *reflect* on the consequences of *his actions.* "If I do this now, what will the consequences be in two weeks, or six months, or two years?" He may decide to abstain from something he wishes to do because although he could gratify himself for the moment, the long term consequences of his action are deleterious. This is something an animal cannot do.

Man has *the capacity to control anger.* When an animal is enraged, it promptly acts out its anger. A person may suppress his anger, and reflect upon whether he wishes to express it at all, and if so, when and how to do so. He may even assess the provocative act and conclude that there is no reason for him to be angry because the person who committed the provocative act did not realize what he was doing or to whom he was doing it. Animals cannot do this.

A person has *the capacity to forgive.* Even if someone did harm him, and even if this was done intentionally, a person may forgive the offender if he so wishes. Man may decide to "forgive but not forget" or may even try to dismiss the entire incident from his mind, whereas animals may or may not forget, but it is highly doubtful that they are capable of forgiving.

Man is the only living creature that can be considered *truly free.* Animals, even in the wild, are not truly free because they are under the absolute domination of their body and cannot make a free choice. If an animal is hungry, it *must* look for food. No hungry animal can decide, "I'm going to fast today." The ability to defy a bodily desire is unique to human beings.

There is only one thing that can prevent an animal from fulfilling a bodily drive, and that is *fear of retribution*. Suppose a hungry jackal is foraging for food and spies a carcass which would satiate his appetite. The carcass, however, is being feasted upon by a huge, ferocious tiger. The jackal makes no attempt to partake of the carcass, not because it does not wish to take what is rightfully the tiger's property, but because it knows that if it attempts to do so it will be killed by the tiger. The fear of retribution overrides the desire for food.

People may sometimes quell a desire because of fear of retribution. A person who works in a financial institution which turns over many millions of dollars each day may be very shrewd in the use of computers, and may be able to transfer sums of money to his own account, becoming very wealthy fairly effortlessly. He is very greedy and has an inordinate desire to be rich. However, he considers that the auditing team undoubtedly has someone who is computer-crime savvy, and if these transactions are traced to him, his ill-begotten money will be taken from him, he will be fined $50,000, and given a 15-year prison sentence. Inasmuch as this is too great a risk to take, he forgoes his greed. In this case, he suppresses his desire only because of fear of retribution, a trait which he shares with lower forms of life.

When is suppression of desire uniquely human? When there is no possibility of detection and retribution, yet the person suppresses a desire and restrains himself only because it is morally and ethically wrong. This is something which animals cannot do. Except when there is fear of retribution, animals are not free to choose whether or not to fulfill a craving, hence they are under the tyranny of their bodies and cannot be said to be truly free. Only man has the capacity to make choices based on morals and ethics, hence man is the only being that can be considered to be truly free, and this trait is therefore one of the defining features of man. There are other features which can be found only in man, which we will be discussing.

Let us take *all* the traits that are unique to man and group them together. The sum total of all these are what I refer to as the *spirit*. The spirit is thus comprised of all the features that are distinctly human and that therefore separate human beings from animals. Unless we extend the term *sapiens* to include all these, we fall far short of a proper definition of humanity if we understand *Homo sapiens* as referring only to intellect.

There is no way one can deny that every human being has these capacities, hence every human being has a spirit. We believe that the spirit was instilled in man by G–d at the time of man's creation. Those who do not believe that G–d created man must nevertheless agree that man has a spirit, but they may contend that these features were somehow developed in the process of human evolution. *That man has a spirit is thus independent of one's belief.*

Man may or may not put these capacities to use. If he does, he is implementing the spirit and can therefore be said to be *spiritual*. There can be varying degrees or levels of spirituality depending on how much one exercises these uniquely human capacities. *Spirituality* is thus nothing more than the implementation of these capacities, hence *spirituality can be seen as being synonymous with humanity*. To the degree that a person is lacking in spirituality, to that degree he is lacking in humanity.

Many of us can recall that as children we were often admonished, "Be a *mentsch*," or "Act like a *mentsch*." Although we walked upright and verbalized words and concepts, we were not yet a "*mentsch*." What was being asked of us is that we develop those traits that are the hallmark of a human being, the spiritual traits that elevate him above the level of *Homo sapiens*. Those who attended a *cheder* where Torah was translated into Yiddish will recall that the translation of *naaseh adam* was "Let us make a *mentsch*." G–d did not merely wish to create "man." Rather, He wished to create a *mentsch*, a spiritual human being.

As can be seen, we have thus far not included religion in the definition of spirituality, hence we may refer to this as a definition of *generic* spirituality. We may now move on to an analysis of *Jewish* spirituality, which is *how a Jew should exercise his uniquely human capacities.*

What About the Body?

efore going on to an elaboration of spirituality, we should spend a moment on the
understanding of the human body. In *mussar* and chassidic writings, there is a term
nefesh habeheimis (animal soul), which indicates that
the physical component of the human being is essentially animal in nature. We differ from animals in that we
possess the spirit component, but our body is really no
different than that of the animal in its desires and impulses. Obviously, we were not meant to function as
animals, and it our task to bring the body under the
mastery of the spirit, but we should understand that it is

part of our being to have animalistic tendencies, many of which we might wish to disown.

The Midrash states that when Moses ascended to heaven to receive the Torah, the angels protested, arguing that mere mortals were not deserving of the Torah, that they were certain to transgress it, and that therefore it should be given to them, i.e., to the Divine angels. G–d then said to Moses, "Rebut their argument." Moses said to the angels, "The Torah says, 'You shall not kill.' Are you capable of killing one another? The Torah says, 'You shall not covet your neighbor's belongings.' Are you capable of desiring something that belongs to another angel?" By enumerating the Torah prohibitions, Moses demonstrated that the Torah can only be given to "mere mortals," because its laws do not apply to and cannot be relevant to angels.

This Midrash tells us that we were given the Torah with its many prohibitions precisely *because we have the desires for the things and acts that are forbidden.* I have always claimed that it is not necessary for me to spend time on a psychoanalyst's couch to discover what impulses may be in my unconscious. I know that there is part of me that may desire and crave all the 365 prohibitions of the Torah. Hence, if I were to discover that I have an impulse for something that is morally reprehensible, I would not be in the least surprised. There are many impulses and drives within me that are part of my physical-animal component, and it is my duty to see that those that the Torah forbids should never be acted upon.

In observance of Torah, we restrain ourselves from its prohibitions, very often by suppressing the unacceptable drives. However, there is also the possibility of channeling these drives toward desirable goals, and rather than simply suppressing them, using their energy for positive accomplishments. This is something that we will discuss a bit later. At any rate, rather than deny and disown the unacceptable drives, which would mean that we are struggling against an unknown enemy, it is preferable to realize that they may exist as part of our animal nature, and since it is our task to rise to spirituality, we must exercise mastery over them.

Learning from the Past

I t is indeed tragic that mankind has failed to implement this uniquely human capacity. How many lives could have been saved, how much misery could have been avoided, if only we had learned from the past. It has rightly been said that "those who do not learn from history are bound to repeat it."

In our Torah literature, from the Pentateuch to the Prophets to the Talmud to contemporary writings, we are repeatedly told that our welfare is dependent upon Torah observance. We are especially reminded of the pivotal role of *ahavas Yisrael*, and that when there is unity amongst us, G–d will overlook even major transgressions. We are told that whereas the First Temple was lost because of grave sins, the people at the time of the Second Temple were observant of Torah, but were bitterly divided, and that this resulted in its destruction. All this knowledge of history notwithstanding, we still allow petty differences and grievances to set us apart from one another. If only we used this precious spiritual gift — the capacity to learn from the past — how different our course of history would have been.

It is one thing, and as we can see, extremely important, to learn from the mistakes of the past, but it is equally important to learn from the greatness of the past, and here is where Judaism parts ways with secularism. Science teaches the theory of evolution, according to which all matter started (somehow) from infinitesimally minute particles, and over many eons more complex organisms developed, eventually culminating in hominoids (ape-like creatures), and then proceeding unto man. According to this theory, every generation is an improvement on the past, and there is little to look back upon with any pride. Certainly modern man, with his unbelievably sophisticated computers, undreamed of medical advances, and the ability to send and retrieve a man from the moon, is a vast improvement over past generations.

In Judaism this is not so. Every ensuing generation is further removed from Adam, the handiwork of G-d. Every generation is more distant from the one which witnessed the revelation at Sinai and heard G-d speak to them. We are expected to say, "When can I ever reach the level of my forefathers?" מעשֹ אֵינֹ

It is of interest that every generation of Torah Jews has looked back upon the preceding generations with great reverence and even awe. In *halachah*, Torah scholars may not dispute the ruling of the scholars of a previous era. Today we look back at the pre-war generation, at such Torah giants as Reb Chaim Ozer, the Chafetz Chaim, and Reb Boruch Ber, and we realize that their greatness is beyond our reach. Reb Boruch Ber related that his master, Reb Chaim of Brisk, would devote considerable time telling of the great people he knew, time that otherwise could have been spent on formal study, because he believed that the very lives of these people were a Torah study. And when Reb Boruch Ber spoke of Reb Chaim, he would tell his students that there was a quantum leap between himself and Reb Chaim, and would exclaim, "My dear students! These eyes were fortunate to have looked upon true *tzaddikim!*" This is the pattern of Jewish thought, essentially evolution in reverse.

This gives us the possibility of learning from our rich heritage, and if we cannot attain the greatness of our forebears, we at least have a standard toward which we can strive. In *Not Just Stories* I related a number of anecdotes about our great men and women of the past who can serve as models for us. What has been preserved for us is but a tiny fragment of their lives, lives which were paragons of total devotion to G–d and fellow man, of brilliant scholarship, of self-sacrifice, and of self-effacement.

Just consider. Rabbi Boruch Ber stood in awe before Reb Chaim, who stood in awe before Rabbi Akiva Eiger and the Gaon of Vilna. They in turn revered the Torah scholars before them. It is related that one of the Vilna

Gaon's students, awed by the master's incomparable brilliance and total command of the entire Torah, compared him to the Rambam. The Gaon shuddered. "How dare one compare anyone of this generation to the Rambam?" he said. Can we then begin to appreciate the greatness of the Rambam and Rashi, and since the latter considered the authors of the Talmud as being infinitely superior to them, what kind of concept can we have about them? This is why the Talmud says, "If the earlier generations were Divine angels, then by comparison we can be considered human beings. If the previous generations are to be considered as human beings, then by comparison we are like donkeys" (*Shabbos* 112b).

I do not wish to repeat stories I have written elsewhere, but will cite just one, which if properly understood gives us an insight into the characters of our great Torah personalities.

R*abbi Akiva Eiger had a number of guests at his Seder, and one guest clumsily tipped his wine goblet, spilling wine onto the tablecloth. Rabbi Akiva Eiger promptly nudged the table with his knee, causing several other goblets to spill, and said, "I'm sorry about this unsteady table. I had been meaning to have it repaired, but did not get around to it." He thus prevented the clumsy guest from being humiliated.*

You may say, "Yes, this was indeed a fine gesture, and indicates the Rabbi's thoughtfulness. But this does not indicate any special greatness."

Ah, then you have missed the point of the story. Had

the Rabbi hesitated even momentarily in nudging the table, it would have been evident to all that the guest's accident had nothing to do with the unsteadiness of the table, and the ruse would have been patent. The reason the Rabbi's gesture was effective is because there was not even a split second delay between the spilling of the first and subsequent cups. Rabbi Akiva Eiger did not have to think for a moment what to do. His motion was immediate, spontaneous, and virtually reflex in nature, occurring as rapidly as the blinking of the eyes at the approach of a flying object. In other words, Rabbi Akiva Eiger's body was poised for automatic and immediate reaction to such situations. To have trained one's system to be reflexively responsive to protect the dignity of another person, that was the greatness of Rabbi Akiva Eiger, and this is the kind of behavior of which our predecessors were capable.

The Talmud is correct. We are *qualitatively* different than previous generations. Even if we cannot aspire to their greatness, we have models whom we can emulate.

Purpose of Existence

e have noted that one of the unique capacities of man is that he can reflect on the purpose of his existence. This is one of the human capacities that has often been allowed to lie fallow. Many (if not most) people go about their lives so engrossed in their daily activities that they hardly give any thought as to why they are doing things. I.e., they obviously know what their short-term goals are — e.g., that they are driving the car in order to get to work, and that they are working in order to earn a wage, etc. — however, they give little thought to what the *ultimate* purpose of their existence is.

It is meaningless to talk of the ultimate purpose of an individual if the entire universe is purposeless. Thus, if one believes in the primacy of matter and/or energy, and that the universe was not created but came into being as a result of some freak accident, then it makes no sense to ask what one's *ultimate* goal in life is. One can indeed have goals such as keeping the world clean, combating acid rain and preserving the tropical forests and endangered species, but there cannot be an ultimate goal in a world which, as a whole, has no goal. It is much like the story of the two vagrants who were brought before the judge. "What were you doing when the officer arrested you?" the judge asked one vagrant. "Nothing," the man answered. "And what were you doing when you were arrested?" the judge asked the second vagrant. "I was helping him," the man answered.

Helping someone who is doing nothing may seem meritorious, but one is actually doing nothing. Similarly, doing things for a world that lacks purpose cannot be purposeful. The only way one can consider the ultimate purpose of one's existence is if the world itself has a purpose, and this presupposes that it was created for a purpose by a Creator.

Belief in a Creator may require a "leap of faith." In spite of all the philosophical arguments that have been proposed throughout history to prove the existence of G–d, the fact is that it is a matter of faith. As Rambam says, "A person is obligated to believe that there is a G–d," and the 13 principles of faith that Rambam cites as the foundation of Judaism are matters of belief. Anything that can be proven is not an object of faith.

One does not have to *believe* that 2 + 2 = 4, nor that a magnet can attract iron filings, because these can be proven beyond the shadow of a doubt. Judaism is predicated on the *belief* that there is a G–d.

However, it is more than mere belief. Judaism has an *uninterrupted* transmission from generation to generation of the revelation at Sinai, where over two million people heard the voice of G–d and witnessed the awe-inspiring scene described in *Exodus*. There was not a single deviation of the account handed down to their children by those present.

Perhaps I have a bit of an advantage. My great-grandfather was the Rebbe of Hornostipol, the *Zeide* Reb Motele. My grandfather was his son, and my father remembered him, as did many of his *chassidim* whom I was privileged to know. The *Zeide* Reb Motele was a Torah scholar without peer, and at age 17 he wrote a masterful work on *halachah*, upon which the great luminary Reb Chaim of Brisk remarked that he did not believe that anyone of this generation could compose such a treatise. His intellectual brilliance was equaled only by his incomparable acts of *chesed*, and from his *chassidim* and from my grandfather I heard stories of his greatness which would have been appropriate for the Baal Shem Tov.

Yes, I have come across philosophical arguments about the existence of G–d. Like many others, I have been bewildered by the suffering of the innocent and righteous, and I have not been able to avoid thinking, "How could G–d permit this to happen?" It is a rare person that never questions his belief. However, I recognize that the *Zeide* Reb Motele was far brighter and far more intelligent than I will ever be, and all the questions that may occur to me certainly occurred to him. Nevertheless, the *Zeide* Reb Motele had an unfaltering conviction in Hashem and Torah, and that is more than adequate for me.

In contrast to things that can be proven, faith is supra-rational. Inasmuch as G–d is infinite and the mind of man is finite, there is simply no way that a human being can understand anything about G–d, other than that which He revealed to us in a manner that we can integrate. All the terms we use to refer to G–d are in essence inaccurate, and we use them only because these are the only vehicles we have for expression and communication. For example, when we say that G–d is compassionate, our natural tendency is to think of compassion the way we know it, i.e., human compassion. The fact is, however, that Divine compassion and human compassion are qualitatively different, and we cannot have a true understanding of what Divine compassion is. Yet, since we need to speak about G–d insofar as He has revealed Himself to us, we can only use the words we have. We must bear in mind, however, that these are essentially "borrowed" terms, as we cannot ascribe to G–d any of the feelings we associate with human experience.

Thus, when we speak of "the will of G–d," we must dissociate this from our concept of will as we understand it. When a human being wants something, he is pleased when he gets whatever it was that he desired, hence there is a change in his feelings. I.e., he is happier after he gets what he wanted than he was before. This cannot be true of G–d, since G–d is all perfect, and never changes in any way. What then do we mean by "the will of G–d?" Only that if G–d does something, it is because it is in keeping with His "will," and if he commands us to do something, it is in keeping with His "will" that we do it. The kabbalists therefore refer to G–d's will with the term "simple will," to indicate that it is distinct from human will and is not associated with a change of feeling the way human will is. It is evident, however, that we are talking about something which is completely beyond our capacity to understand.

We believe that G–d created the universe, and that He has a purpose for its existence. We believe that G–d gave us the Torah to reveal to us how we are to participate in that purpose. Again, since G–d cannot be "happier" after creation of the universe than before, the idea that He had a "purpose" is beyond our comprehension. It is in matters such as this that we are told: "Do not seek to understand those things that are beyond you" (*Chagigah* 13a).

In geometry there are some principles or axioms which are its foundations, as, for example, that two parallel lines cannot intersect, or that quantities which are equal to the same quantity are equal to each other. Once we assume these principles and axioms, we can then build an entire structure of geometry on them. Similarly, once we accept the principles of faith, we can then use our intellect to build upon them, but the basic principles are givens. We cannot ask *why* G–d has this purpose for the universe or *why* he has this purpose for us as individuals. We can only build upon the principles He has revealed to us in the Torah, and, using the tools revealed to us for Torah study, elaborate upon those principles.

There are many works in Torah literature that address the question of man's purpose in life. One of the most lucid presentations is that of RaMCHaL (Luzzatto) in his epochal work, *Path of the Just* (*Mesillas Yesharim*). RaMCHaL states that the ultimate purpose of man's existence is to be in the immanent presence of the revealed glory of G–d, and that this can only occur in the eternal, heavenly world. However, man can achieve this goal only by appropriately preparing himself for it in this earthly world, by performing the mitzvos which G–d commanded. RaMCHaL states, and this is further elaborated in *Tanya*, that the gap between mortal man and infinite G–d is unbridgeable except via the Divine commandments. No method developed by man can bridge this gap. Thus, neither seeking unification with the universe via meditation nor, as some have unfortunately thought, by mind-expanding chemicals, can man be brought close to G–d.

Observing the Divine mitzvos in this world can indeed bring a person close to G–d, but the ultimate bliss of being in the immanent presence of G–d cannot be reached as long as the soul is confined within the physical body. This ultimate goal can therefore be achieved only after one's earthly existence has come to an end, but one must utilize the earthly existence in order to gain access to the eternal world.

Man should not delude himself into thinking that the ultimate purpose of existence can be in this world, and certainly not that he was created to indulge in all the earthly pleasures available to him. The Talmud indeed states that G–d wishes us to enjoy the world (*Jerusalem Talmud,* end of *Kiddushin*), but this is while we are en route to fulfilling our ultimate purpose.

Western civilization seems to have adopted a hedonistic philosophy of life. In recent times the advance of science and technology has produced near miraculous achievements, so that the average life span has been dramatically prolonged, and countless devices have made living much more comfortable. Yet, it is evident, as RaMCHaL points out, that man could not have been created merely for the purpose of reaching contentment in life, because if this were the case, endowing him with great intellect defeats the purpose. Lower forms of life experience far less distress than man, whose superior brain, while allowing him to write great literature, compose musical masterpieces, and develop highly sophisticated computers, also renders him susceptible to anxiety, stress, and painful emotional disorders which do not plague lower forms of life. As RaMCHaL so correctly points out, once we believe that G–d created man, it is absurd to think that it was for man to be content, because the lives of the overwhelming majority of humans are replete with suffering. "You will not find one out of a thousand for whom the world has provided pleasure and tranquility" (*Mesillas Yesharim,* Chapter 1). It is of great interest and extreme importance that the "one out of a thousand" who appears to have pleasure and tranquility may not be satisfied with this, and this may well be the primary reason why many people have turned to a Torah life. Sometimes they just feel an inexplicable void and embark on a search for meaning. At other times a significant event stimulates and initiates this search. Let me cite an example of the latter.

T he first thing I saw at medical school was a dead man. From that first day in the anatomy dissection hall as I peeled back the heavy sheet from the cadaver I was to dissect, everything seemed different. I had begun to wonder about purpose and meaning, and delving into that human body daily, discovering its wonders and simultaneously facing death, exposed a vague emptiness; he seemed to be challenging me, demanding that I examine myself and define where I was going. He had been a young man; the label on the sheet said: "Cause of death unknown," and in a way he was me. Even the best medical school teaches only sophisticated plumbing, really, and does not answer the existential questions; if anything it raises them, presents paradoxes: Man is an accidental creature distantly descended from an amoeba and closely related to an ape, and yet his life is worth saving. It did not make any sense.

I had never thought much beyond myself until then: I had not been searching for anything in particular, and the question of ultimate meaning had never really bothered me, probably because my life in the day-to-day present had been so full. I had grown up in the lap of South African luxury and lacked nothing: money, servants who did everything from polishing shoes to serv-

ing breakfast in bed, weekends on the tennis court and by the pool, holidays on the Cape's breathtaking beaches or on safari in the national game parks, endless entertainment; in short, all the gracious ease that was South Africa. I owned three motorcycles before I was 18, and an Italian convertible ... I had everything I wanted and enjoyed it all (Anatomy of a Search, Mesorah Publications, 1987).

The author goes on to relate how the search for meaning brought him and a number of his friends to Torah. One young man who consulted me was not so fortunate. He too had everything he wanted and enjoyed it all, but was plagued by the feeling of emptiness described above. Instead of turning to spirituality, he found his solution in drugs, and while heroin indeed temporarily relieved his distress over feeling empty, his addiction led to his self-destruction.

Man's ultimate purpose can therefore not be found in this earthly world.

RaMCHaL goes on to explain that man's task on earth is to fulfill the Divine mitzvos and to withstand the various trials and tests to which he is put. The moments of tranquility and pleasure that he has are merely "rest stops," as it were, to enable him to recharge his energies for the ongoing struggle,

Man's soul is totally spiritual, a Divine entity which G–d gave to man. This soul, which strives for spiritual delights, is housed in a physical and essentially animal body, whose strivings are anathema to the soul. Yet, the only way that the soul can reach its coveted position in the eternal world is via the mitzvos, which can only be performed by a physical body. The soul wishes to direct the body toward its goals, whereas the cravings inherent within man's animal body are in direct contradiction to the soul's aspirations; hence there is a fierce struggle between body and soul, a struggle in which man is engaged throughout his entire lifetime. In order to assist man in his task of fulfilling the mitzvos, RaMCHaL discusses the *middos* (character traits) which are conducive to man's mission and those which detract therefrom.

A somewhat different approach is taken by chassidic philosophy, which states that G–d wished to have a presence in the physical world. Again, we are at a total loss to understand why G–d would wish this, but as pointed out earlier, we cannot understand anything about the nature of G–d's will.

The Divine presence in the earthly world is brought about by the performance of mitzvos. Since the latter requires material objects, e.g., parchment for Torah and *mezuzos,* leather for *tefillin,* an *esrog* (citron) for Succos, etc., these mundane objects are transformed into spiritual items of *kedushah* (holiness). Similarly, when one utilizes the energy gained from eating food to perform mitzvos, the food which enables this performance is elevated to *kedushah.* Since a person cannot function optimally without proper clothing and shelter or without the funds to acquire the necessities of life, everything that he does can be transformed into objects or acts of *kedushah,* and this brings about the Divine presence in the physical world, which is the ultimate purpose of man.

In *Tanya*, Rabbi Shneur Zalman of Liadi states that man's purpose is to discover the truth of all existence, which is that everything in the universe exists only because of a spark of Divinity within it. He points out that there is a tendency for all things to remain in their natural state unless there is a strong enough force to drive them from it. For example, the natural state of a stone lying on the ground is to remain there by the force of gravity, unless lifted by a force that exceeds the gravitational pull. If someone throws the stone high into the air, it will continue to rise only as long as the force of the thrower exceeds the gravitational pull. Once this force is exhausted, the stone returns to rest on the ground again.

Since there was nothing in existence prior to Creation, the natural state of the universe is nothingness. It required a force to bring the world into existence, and this force was the command of G–d for everything to come into being. If this force were ever exhausted, the universe would disappear into nothingness again. Creation was thus not a single historical incident, but is essentially an ongoing process. Rabbi Shneur Zalman points out that whereas an object fashioned by a craftsman continues to exist after it has left his hands, this is because the material from which the object was formed was in existence without the craftsman, and he merely altered its shape. This is different than the universe coming out of nothingness, which requires a sustaining force to keep it in existence.

Within everything on earth, from the largest to the most miniscule, there is a spark of Divinity which maintains it in existence. This Divine spark is concealed by the physical object it inhabits, and if man's perception were pure, he would see this Divine spark. The physical objects thus mask the reality of G–d's presence in everything. Since everything is totally effaced in the Divine presence, the only true reality is G–d, but in order for us to function as mortals, we see the objects as though they had an independent existence. Man's purpose is to penetrate the cloaks of concealment and recognize the true reality. Thus, Rabbi Shneur Zalman says, the last phrase of the verse in the Torah which states that "G–d is the Lord in the heavens above and on the earth below, there is no other," (*Deuteronomy* 4:39) should better be read "there is nothing else." The only true existence is G–d.

It is related that the chassidic master, Rabbi Mendel of Rimanov, was walking with his disciples, when they came across a crying child. "Why are you crying?" Rabbi Mendel asked. "Because we are playing hide and seek. I hid myself, but none of the children is trying to find me." Rabbi Mendel turned to his disciples and said, "Can you imagine the anguish of G–d, Who concealed Himself within the physical world, but no one is trying to find Him!"

The kabbalists state that "It is the intent of the good to do good," and inasmuch as G–d is the ultimate of goodness, He created the universe in order that there be recipients of His goodness. This, then, is the purpose behind Creation, and man's purpose is to be the recipient of that goodness. This ties in with RaMCHaL's position, because the greatest good that man can attain is to be in the Divine presence in the eternal world. However, since something that is not earned cannot be fully enjoyed, and receiving undeserved reward may actually be uncomfortable and would therefore not be the greatest good, G–d designed the world in a manner that would enable man to earn his reward.

This approach requires a profound trust and belief in Divine benevolence. As we witness the enormous amount of suffering that occurs on earth, we may find it difficult to believe that man was created to receive Divine benevolence. The suffering and atrocities inflicted on people by others may be explained by the fact that man has free will, and that G–d does not intervene to prevent evil people from acting out their evil intent. However, there is also much suffering that is not due to human free will, such as painful and incurable diseases, earthquakes, tornadoes, and other "acts of G–d" in which we are hard pressed to find any good. Yet, our highly spiritual people did just that, as exemplified by Nachum Ish Gamzu, who was able to accept all suffering as being good (*Taanis* 21a).

Few of us can reach the level of faith and trust of Nachum Ish Gamzu, but we may be capable of understanding why we cannot do so. Think of this scenario: A person who has never heard of physicians, medical treatment, and surgery, happens to wander into an operating room. There he sees a helpless person lying on the table, surrounded by masked people, one of whom appears to be suffocating him by covering his nose and mouth, while the others are cutting him open and appear to be dismembering him. Enraged by this unspeakable torture, he may attack this "team of hoodlums" in order to save the "victim." He has no way of knowing that what he perceives to be pure evil and torture is actually a lifesaving procedure. Likewise, with our limited human perception we cannot see any good in the happenings which appear to us to be evil rather than good.

The mystery of human suffering cannot be satisfactorily resolved. The Talmud quotes Rabbi Meir as saying that Moses wished to understand this, but G–d did not reveal it to him (*Berachos* 7a). According to one opinion in the Talmud, Moses wrote the Book of *Job* (*Bava Basra* 14b), where this vexing question is discussed, and all explanations for why bad things happen to good people are rebutted.

It has been said that if one believes in G–d, human suffering does not need to make any sense. If one does not believe in G–d, nothing makes any sense.

There are variations on the themes of the purpose of Creation and that of human existence in the Torah literature, and the common denominator is that man can achieve his ultimate purpose only by following the Divine commandments. This is the Jewish answer to the question raised by exercising the unique human capacity of searching for meaning in one's life.

In *Dearer than Life* (*Mesorah Publications,* 1997) I pointed out that for any thinking person, a life devoid of meaning is intolerable. We can thus see the inadequacy of the appellation *Homo sapiens* as defining man. A person may have superior intellect and may have acquired an enormous fund of knowledge. He may even have composed important works, but if he lacks an ultimate *transcendental* purpose, and sees no goal in life other than personal gratification, he is lacking in an important component of humanity. We therefore have the Torah concept of *mesiras nefesh*, of willingness to give up personal gratification in pursuit of the ultimate purpose of life.

It is the willingness to endure self-sacrifice for a higher goal that gives life meaning. The Talmud relates that when Rabbi Akiva was being tortured to death, his disciples asked, "Master, is this the desired goal?" to which Rabbi Akiva responded, "All my life I have aspired to this" (*Berachos* 61a), by which he meant that it was not the act of martyrdom per se that gives meaning to life, because many people who led rather inane lives accepted martyrdom when their loyalty to G–d was challenged. Rather, it is the *aspiration* to offer oneself up for the glory of G–d that makes life purposeful. It is this aspiration which indicates that one has assigned the participation in earthly activities to its proper place, and that one indeed has an ultimate, transcendent goal.

Self - Improvement

A s was noted, a major distinguishing feature between humans and animals is that animals are created in a state of completion, and their growth is essentially in size and strength. Their maturation follows a life cycle which is instilled within them, and any changes which may occur are the result of their genetic composition. Animals are unable, by volition, to make any material changes in themselves.

Man has the capacity to make changes in himself. He is not an unalterable product of his genetic makeup. There is little doubt that some people harbor inborn character traits and that there is a variation in peoples' innate emotional and intellectual endowment. However, in contrast to animals, man is not helpless insofar as his character is concerned, and he can make salutary changes in himself, even radical changes.

The fact that a person has the capacity to make changes in his character is not sufficiently appreciated by some psychologists, who tend to attribute a person's problems to factors beyond one's control. It is common practice to take a detailed history from a patient, particularly about the various circumstances of his upbringing, which is certainly a necessity in getting to understand a person. However, when faults are discovered in the parents' handling of the patient in early life, the blame for the patient's current problems is often laid at the feet of the parents. While the effects of parenting on one's emotional development cannot be minimized, this approach too often results in a "pity-party," with the patient bewailing the unfairness of his lot in life and essentially resigning himself to dysfunction rather than trying to improve things. Not infrequently, a patient may remain fixated at this level and not take the necessary steps to improve himself. It is much easier to assign blame rather than to change oneself.

A much more constructive approach has been adopted by more modern schools of psychology, which can be summarized as, "Even if you are what your parents made you, if you stay that way it's your own fault." This approach does not deny the importance of early life experiences, but instead of emphasizing their role in the patient's current problems, urges him to make the necessary changes that will remedy them. The human character is not cast in stone, and is not an unalterable product of genetic composition and/or early life experiences.

Tiferes Yisrael (Kiddushin 4:14 §77) cites a Midrash which relates that a king had heard of the greatness of Moses, and was curious to know more about him. He therefore dispatched his artists to the Israelite encampment to draw a picture of Moses. Upon their return he gave the portrait to his physiognomists, who were able to determine a person's character by studying his facial features. The physiognomists submitted their analysis: This person was vain, arrogant, greedy, indolent, irascible, and lustful. The king reprimanded his artists for their incompetence in properly depicting Moses, since there could not be so great a discrepancy between the analysis of his wise men and the accounts he had received of Moses' stellar personality. When the artists swore that their drawing was accurate, the king decided to see for himself.

Upon meeting Moses, the king saw that the artists had not omitted even a single hair. Knowing the reliability of his wise men, the king was perplexed, and confronted Moses with his problem. Moses explained, "Your physiognomists were not mistaken. You see, all that they can deduce from a person's facial features are his inborn traits, and indeed, I was born with all the contemptible character traits they described.

However, I worked to transform them and to become the person that I felt I should be."

This Midrash says it all. We can be whatever we wish to be. Of course, a person who is tone deaf cannot become a cantor, and there are some talents which one either has or does not have, but insofar as *middos* (character traits) are concerned, we have the ability to mold ourselves into whatever we wish to be. The human being thus has the capacity to improve himself.

But what do we mean by improvement? What are the standards and measures of "better"?

We cannot talk about gradations of good unless we know an item's function. Thus, we can say that one automobile is better than another, because the better one can provide faster, more comfortable, and more reliable transportation. It is meaningless, however, to say that an automobile is an improvement on a clock, since their functions are so diverse. The finest automobile cannot tell you what time it is, nor can the finest timepiece transport you to where you wish to be.

Self-improvement presupposes that we know what the function of a person is. If his function is dependent on his physical prowess, then self-improvement will consist of increasing his muscular strength. If his function is to amass great wealth, then he will see self-improvement as consisting of acquiring the business knowledge and cunning that will enable him to make a great deal of money. It is evident that implementing the capacity of self-improvement is dependent on what one accepts as one's goal in life, in which case the desired changes are those that will enhance one's reaching that goal. Having established that according to all concepts, the ultimate goal of a Jew is achieved via performance of mitzvos, self-improvement will consist of those changes that will enhance performance of mitzvos.

The Torah states that the Israelites received the manna prior to the giving of the Torah at Sinai. One of the commentaries explains that the miracle of the manna was that each person could gather only as much as he actually needed. If someone collected more than his needs, the excess would rot. If he collected less, the measure would fill on its own. This was to teach them that G–d will provide everyone with the proper amount for his well-being, and that trying to get more than one's due is futile. Only after this principle was established could the Israelites receive the Torah, which prohibits any unjust acquisition of another person's property. Without this basic *emunah* (belief and trust in G–d), they could not have been expected to obey the commandments against stealing, swearing falsely, taking usury, coveting others' belongings, and all the other mitzvos relating to property rights.

The trait of *emunah* is thus essential for observance of all the mitzvos that involve commerce and property rights. This is equally true of other traits which are conducive to proper performance of mitzvos. Self-improvement therefore consists of developing and perfecting these traits, and eliminating those traits that impede proper performance of mitzvos.

We are fortunate in having a rich repository of Torah literature on the cultivation of proper *middos*. Foremost among these are *Pirkei Avos* (*Ethics of the Fathers*), *Mesillas Yesharim* (*Path of the Just*), and *Orchos Tzaddikim* (*Ways of the Righteous*). These are all available in English. There are also a number of excellent books by contemporary Torah scholars, some of which have been translated into English, such as *Michtav MeEliyahu* (*Strive for Truth*).

It is important to be aware that Torah values differ greatly from secular values. We should also know that there is no way to totally escape the impact of the values that prevail in the environment in which we live, and that inasmuch as these often conflict with Torah values, we must be on our guard not to be influenced by them.

For example, the prevailing cultural concept is that wealth consists of having a great deal of money, and furthermore, that wealth is acquired by diligence and effort at making money. If the average person were asked whom he considers as wealthy, he would undoubtedly name several billionaires, and if asked how they managed to become wealthy, he would respond that they were innovative, had a thorough understanding of economics, were shrewd in business dealings, etc. Torah teaches that the truly wealthy person is one who is content with whatever he has (*Ethics of the Fathers* 4:1); hence a person who barely has enough to survive but is happy with his lot is in fact wealthier than the billionaire who tries to amass more riches and lives in anxiety that an unexpected turn of events might topple him from his lofty position. Furthermore, the Torah warns against thinking that a person becomes wealthy as a result of his own efforts. Many people may try the same thing, yet only one becomes wealthy. This is because a person's fortune is decreed by G–d, and while it is necessary that a person do something to earn a livelihood, it is the Divine blessing that will enrich him (*Deuteronomy* 8:11-18).

Just as wealth is defined differently by Torah than by the culture, so are other values, such as wisdom, honor, power, etc. (*Ethics of the Fathers* 4:1). The Torah values are those that are conducive to the performance of mitzvos, whereas secular values are often antagonistic thereto.

We must also bear in mind that secular values are often determined by the same standards we apply to economics; i.e., success or failure, profit or loss. While the latter are appropriate in commerce, they have no place in morals or ethics. An ethical person is one who tries his utmost to do what is right, with honesty and integrity, and if these efforts fail to produce the desired results, he is nevertheless a good person. On the other hand, a person who violates the principles of decency yet achieves great success is an unethical person. Parents who do their utmost to raise a child with love and good training are good parents even if their child grows up to be a criminal, whereas parents who were self-indulgent and grossly neglected their children are bad parents, even if their child grows up to be a Nobel prize winner. Since we cannot control outcome, we must judge ethics and morality by how and why we act, and not by how things turn out.

Finally, secular values are often determined by courts and legislatures, which may establish laws that they feel to be expedient and beneficial to society. This leaves the door wide open for adoption of even the most corrupt and evil practices into law, as was so dramatically exemplified in the Holocaust, where eliminating Jews was considered to be good for the state, hence a virtuous act. According to Torah, morals and ethics are not subject to cultural desires. Whatever constituted murder or immorality several thousand years ago continues to remain an abomination even if the courts and legislatures rule otherwise.

As we will see, our judgments can be distorted by self-interest, and this is true of society as a whole as well as the individual person. Self-interest may be antagonistic to spirituality; hence true spiritual values are those revealed by G–d in the Torah, and are absolute and immutable. The standards for self-improvement necessary for spiritual development are the unalterable values established by Torah.

Emerging from Confusion

here is nothing that can so disable a person from finding his way to his goal as confusion. Think of a trip you have taken. You follow the road map to your destination, but at one point the road is closed and you must take a detour. Unfortunately, the signs for the detour were not posted well and fell down. You are now off the road, and with the absence of signs as to how to get back on it, you are totally confused. If you proceed in one direction, you may be going away from your destination instead of toward it, and you do not have the faintest idea what to do. As anyone who has experienced this knows, it is a terrible feeling. If someone drives by, you try to flag him down, because perhaps he may know which is the right way. Perhaps you may figure out from the position of the sun at that time of the day which way is east and which way is west. What you are looking for is anything that can help you clear up the confusion.

The path in life is no different. There is a great deal of confusion, and unless someone shows us the right direction, we may be heading away from our goal instead of toward it.

In the account of Creation we are told that G–d separated light from darkness, and the Midrash remarks that prior to this separation, light and darkness were intermingled. This is a difficult concept to understand, because light and darkness cannot possibly coexist. What we may gather from this, however, is that it is possible for two opposites to coexist and be so intermingled that only G–d Himself can separate the two. In our lives we may encounter many admixtures of "light and dark," i.e., good and evil, and we may find ourselves unable to extract the good and leave the evil behind. Only the word of G–d can help us do this.

After the separation, light and darkness were no longer intertwined. "Good" was pure and manifest good, and "evil" was pure and manifest evil. This state of clarity persisted only until Adam and Eve ate of the Tree of Wisdom, whose fruit enabled them to "distinguish good from evil." Prior to their sin there had been no need to distinguish good from evil, because the two were distinct. It was due to Adam's sin that good and evil again became intermingled, and since then man must use his intellect to distinguish between the two. This has remained man's formidable challenge to this very day.

Distinguishing good from evil when they are so interwoven requires a keen sense of judgment. Unfortunately, our capacity to judge correctly is often impaired when a decision involves a personal interest. When one decision will be more to our liking than another, we may be "bribed" by our desire, and our determination of what is good and what is evil may be faulty.

A chassid of the Rabbi of Rhizhin once asked the master for a guideline to help him choose correctly between right and wrong. The Rabbi responded, "The way a tightrope walker maintains his balance is by leaning a bit to the side opposite the one to which he feels himself pulled. You may rest assured that most of your cravings are the work of the yetzer hara. Therefore, when you feel yourself attracted to doing something, you should lean a bit to the other side first and steer away from it. You will then be in a much better position to make an accurate judgment."

The admixture of good and evil can be understood in yet another way. The *yetzer hara* has the power to deceive us by making the evil appear as if it were good, much like covering a poisonous food with a candy coating. It also has the power to delude us and distort our thinking.

Rabbi Shneur Zalman says that every Jew has an instinctive desire to be one with G–d, and that this is a heritage of the Patriarchs. He points out that at the time of the Inquisition, Jews who were not observant of Torah and mitzvos chose to die at the stake rather than reject their faith and deny G–d. This is because they felt that rejecting their faith would cause a break in the bond between them and G–d, and they did not wish to live without a close relationship with G–d.

How is it, then, that these people did not observe Torah? It is because they did not understand that the only contact we can have with G–d is via Torah and mitzvos. Like some people today, they felt that they can be a "Jew at heart," and they were not aware that it is not enough to be a "Jew at heart," and that observance of Torah is the only way a close relationship can exist. This is due to the power of the *yetzer hara* to delude people and make them believe that they can still have a close relationship with G–d even if they are not observant of Torah.

The Talmud (*Sotah* 3a) states that a person does not sin unless he has taken leave of his senses (mind). This is because a well-functioning mind would reason that there is no way that finite man can have an intimate relationship with infinite G–d other than by the method designed by G–d, which is observance of the mitzvos. If a person knew that by violating the Shabbos, dealing dishonestly in business, or committing any other transgression of Torah he severs the bonds that tie him to G–d, he would never commit any transgression. It is only because the *yetzer hara* deludes a person into thinking that the intimate relationship with G–d is not affected by sin, that a person can be seduced to commit sin. A person who willingly accepts martyrdom because he does not wish to break his bond with G–d would be most certain not to fracture that bond by committing any sin, and if he does sin it is because he is not aware that sin weakens his ties to G–d. The Talmud uses the expression, "It is like cutting off the head of the chicken and expecting it not to die" (*Shabbos* 75a). Thinking that one can violate G–d's commandments and still maintain a close bond with G–d is not different.

Inasmuch as a spiritual person is always seeking an ever closer relationship with G–d, he is always on the alert for the wiles of the *yetzer hara*, and aware that the latter may delude him into thinking that evil is good and that wrong is right.

Aggression

As we have noted in our discussion of truth and falsehood, a spiritual person constantly seeks to advance the traits that are uniquely human and to elevate himself above the animal component of his being. He would certainly avoid anything that might lower him beneath the animal level.

Animals are aggressive, but, as a rule, will not kill any of their own species. Studies of animal aggression against their own species indicate that this is for one reason only: to protect against encroachment upon the animal's territory. Individual animals do this for themselves, and a group of animals may do this for the entire group.

If humans act this way, it would be descending to an animal level. For humans to go beyond this, and kill members of their own species, is descending far below an animal level.

A chassid once complained to Rabbi Mendel of Rimanov that someone had opened a competing business near his, and he was afraid that his income would be diminished. Rabbi Mendel told him that when a horse drinks from a stream, it taps with its foot. This is because when it sees its reflection in the water, it thinks that there is another horse there, and that the latter may drink all the water. Consequently, it taps with its foot to chase this other horse away.

A person should have better judgment than this. Judaism teaches that a person's earnings are predetermined on Rosh Hashanah, and no one can detract from whatever has been allotted for a person.

The Baal Shem Tov thought that those very traits that we see as essentially animal in nature can be redirected towards spiritual goals. He therefore said that these traits need not be disowned and repressed, but transformed and converted. There is great psychological wisdom in this approach. In psychology, there is a concept of "sublimation," which is a process whereby the mind converts an unacceptable drive to an acceptable one, generally by altering the goal. According to this theory, a scientist whose curiosity leads him to peer through a telescope or a microscope has converted a voyeuristic impulse to one of scientific curiosity. The problem with this type of sublimation is that it is an unconscious process, and the person has no idea that this is occurring. The unconscious mind has intervened to shield the person from struggling with unacceptable impulses. If the impulses were not sublimated, they would have to be totally repressed, and this would occur at a cost of great expenditure of psychic energy, whereas sublimation allows the repressed emotion to emerge in a disguised fashion.

However, sublimation does not totally eliminate repression. It is much like having a closed container in which steam is being generated. The increasing force of the steam would cause the container to burst, but if someone punctures just a tiny hole in the container, this serves as a safety valve to allow enough steam to escape so that the container remains intact. In this situation, there is still much steam under pressure, and the lid of the container must be kept on tightly.

Unconscious sublimation is essentially a safety valve which allows the repressed impulse to be sufficiently vented in disguised form so that the psyche is not overwhelmed. While sublimation is indeed helpful, it does not do away with the need to continue repressing the impulse. What the Baal Shem Tov advocated is *conscious* rather than *unconscious* sublimation. Instead of disowning an impulse because it is reprehensible, a person should recognize it as a normal component of his animal nature, and realize that if he were an animal, expression of the impulse would be normal. It is because he is a human being that he may not act-out such impulses but rather redirect them toward an acceptable goal.

Aggression against another person is reprehensible. However, there is much injustice that prevails in the world, and a spiritual person should seek to eliminate injustice, even when he is not personally affected. Evil, wrongdoing, and injustice are things which exist in the world, and eliminating them requires that we conduct war against them. A person should therefore allow himself to be aware of his aggressive impulses, but to channel them to battling against those things that should be eliminated.

A true self-awareness of one's psychological and emotional makeup and a conscious effort at rechanneling improper impulses may eliminate the need for repression.

In reviewing the lives of our great Torah personalities, it is nothing less than amazing to note the inordinate amount of energy they invested in Torah study and performance of mitzvos. Many of them functioned well on just a subsistence level of sleep and nourishment, something which we might consider impossible for ourselves. In all likelihood, they were able to consciously sublimate the animal aspect of their being, hence they were free of repression, and were therefore able to use the enormous amount of psychic energy for Torah study. Even if we cannot achieve this level of excellence, it can serve as a model which we should emulate.

Chesed

The unique human capacity to do *chesed* (acts of kindness), even at the cost of one's own comfort, is the cornerstone of Judaism. The father of our people, the patriarch Abraham, is most noted for his acts of *chesed*. At the advanced age of 99, just three days after his circumcision, he sat at the door of his tent in the sweltering heat of the day, looking for wayfarers for whom he might provide food, water, and respite from their wearying travel. Additionally, we are taught that the world was created for the purpose of *chesed* (*Psalms* 89:3). Torah commentaries are unanimous in exalting *chesed*. *Gemilas chasadim* is the greatest of all mitzvos (*Maharsha, Succah* 49b). "Anyone who goes to bed thinking, 'Tomorrow I shall arise and do a kindness to someone,' is assured that he will rejoice with the *tzaddikim* in the World to Come (*Yalkut, Proverbs,* Chapter 12).

The *Shevet Mussar* explains the extraordinary importance of *chesed*. If, indeed, a person dedicates himself sincerely to *chesed,* it should lead him to observance of all of Torah. Why? Because the Talmud says that a person should think of himself as having an equal number of mitzvos and sins, and should think of the world as being comprised of an equal number of *tzaddikim* and *resha'im* (evildoers). Since each individual is judged according to the majority of his acts, and since the entire world is judged according to the majority of its populace, if he does one mitzvah, he now has more mitzvos than sins and is considered to be a *tzaddik*. And if there is one more *tzaddik,* it tips the balance of the world into favor, because there are now more *tzaddikim* than *resha'im*. With a single mitzvah a person can therefore redeem the entire world. The converse is true if he commits a sin (*Kiddushin* 40b). Therefore, says *Shevet Mussar,* a person who is devoted to *chesed* will never allow himself to be the one who would cause a harsh judgment against the entire world. His benevolence would make him bring the world into a favorable position. Hence, a person of *chesed* would never sin (Chapter 30).

Rabbi Dessler states that acts of *chesed* bring about a greater *ahavas Yisrael*. He points out an important psychological fact: It is not that you give to those whom you love, but, to the contrary, you love those to whom you give. When you give something to someone, regardless of whether it is in the form of substance or a favor, you are actually investing something of yourself in him, and because there is the natural tendency to foster and protect your investment, you develop a positive feeling toward any recipient of your *chesed*. Inasmuch as the love of a fellow man is of primary importance in Torah, the pivotal role of *chesed* can be appreciated (*Michtav MeEliyahu,* Volume 1).

Inasmuch as the distinguishing features between the drives of the human spirit and those of the physical body are that the former are centrifugal (directed outward, toward others) and the latter centripetal (directed to self-gratification), *chesed* may be considered to be a measure of spirituality. One might conceivably ask, "If acts of *chesed* are the key to spirituality, and if our goal is to be spiritual, then why must I observe all the ritual mitzvos? Is it not enough that I do much *chesed?* What do I gain spiritually by observing Shabbos, *kashrus* and all the other mitzvos?"

Although *chesed* can indeed be considered the key to spirituality, it does not constitute the whole of it. As we have seen, there are a number of other traits that comprise spirituality, and many of these represent a suppression of various animalistic drives. Secondly, the mitzvos are the only bridge between man and G–d, and for whatever reason G–d designed these specific acts as the way to reach Him, the fact is that they are the only bond available, and one cannot expect an intimate relationship with G–d if one neglects the Divine mitzvos.

Thirdly, one cannot claim to be proficient in *chesed* if one fails to observe all the mitzvos. *Chesed* is contingent upon being sensitive to the needs of others, and transgression of the mitzvos may interfere with the sensitivity requisite for *chesed*. For example, we find that consuming non-kosher foods dulls one's sensitivities (*Shulchan Aruch, Yoreh Deah* 81:7), and one can hardly do adequate *chesed* if one's sensitivities are dull. In a response to some philosophers, Rambam says, "It is evident from your argument that you had just eaten *tereifah*," meaning that Rambam recognized that their thought processes had been distorted by the *tereifah* foods they had consumed. In an age when we are keenly aware of how minute quantities of a chemical can radically alter the way a person thinks and feels, the fact that *tereifah* foods may impact on one's emotions is readily understandable. Obviously, a person whose sensitivities have been compromised may think that he is doing adequate *chesed,* while in fact this may be far from the truth.

Finally, what may appear to be acts of *chesed* may sometimes be self-serving, and if so, they are centripetal rather than centrifugal, and contribute little to spirituality. The Talmud states that Rabbi Yochanan ben Zakkai asked his students to interpret the phrase, "The *chesed* of the nations is lacking" (*Proverbs* 14:34), and each of them gave an example of how kings and governments did things which did indeed benefit the populace, but they did them for their own aggrandizement rather than primarily for the good of the populace. I.e., they wished to reinforce their position of control by gaining the loyalty of the populace, or wished to have their names perpetuated in public works. Although any action which benefits others is commendable even if it is done to gratify one's ego, it is an imperfect *chesed,* one which is lacking in quality.

The Talmud enumerates various categories of *tzedakah,* the finest being when it is given in such a manner that the donor does not know the identity of the recipient, and the recipient is not aware of who the donor is. This type of *tzedakah* shields the recipient from any humiliation, and since it does not provide any acclaim or expression of gratitude for the donor, it is purely altruistic and is not in any way egocentric.

The *tzedakah* of the *tzaddik* of Sanz was legendary, and he was so concerned that the poor should receive the help they needed, that he encouraged people to give abundantly, even if they wished to receive public praise for their philanthropy. While all kinds of *tzedakah* and *chesed* are indeed praiseworthy, they do not generate the quality of spiritual growth as do purely altruistic acts. By fulfilling all the mitzvos of the Torah, especially those which we do not understand and we do purely out of deference to the Divine will, we subject our personal interest to the will of G–d. This diminishes our egocentricity, and enables us to do *chesed* purely because it is the Divine will rather than for our personal interests.

I*t is related that a tzaddik once came upon a poor family, and he gave them substantial tzedakah. A bit later he returned and gave them some more money. He explained, "When I saw the hungry children, their suffering caused me* *great anguish, and when I gave them tzedakah, I felt relieved of my distress at their plight. Thus, my tzedakah was tainted with self-interest. I then returned to give them tzedakah again, but this time it was solely to fulfill the mitzvah, since my discomfort had already been relieved.*

Thus, while all *tzedakah* and *chesed* are mitzvos, the growth in spirituality is related to the purity of the mitzvah.

There are certain types of *chesed* which require very careful analysis, and the determination of the efficacy of these types of *chesed* should be made by consulting a competent authority rather than by relying on one's own judgment.

There are times when what may seem to be acts of *chesed* are actually harmful. A classic example is one which I encounter regularly in my work in treating addiction, when people who try to be "kind" to the addict actually encourage his addiction. Thus, parents who continue to give their child money, even though he is using drugs, are hardly being kind to him. The family member who covers the debts of an addictive gambler in order to avoid his going to jail for fraud is not being kind to him. The person who uses his influence to extricate a friend from a drunk-driving charge is not being kind to him. In all such instances, one may think he is doing the subject a favor, while by relieving him of the unpleasant consequences of his addictive behavior, he is actually removing the distress which might bring the person to his senses and make him aware of the need for help to overcome his addiction.

In our profession we must often recommend "tough love," which is similar to the love of a mother who has her infant child immunized. She indeed allows the doctor to hurt the child with an injection, and she knows that the infant will suffer 48 hours of fever and misery, but because of her true love of her child, she allows him to be hurt to protect him from crippling and deadly diseases. This is a prototype for "tough love." How foolish it would be if a mother wished to "protect" her child from the painful ordeal of immunization, and thereby put him at serious risk of developing untreatable diseases! Such "kindness" is certainly misguided, and is anything but kindness.

We must be careful that the *chesed* we do is not of the kind that promotes harm. Inasmuch as we are invariably emotionally involved with a loved one, we should seek objective counseling, to make sure that we are not blinded by our emotions to the degree that we engage in misguided kindness.

Jewish spirituality is based entirely on Torah, and the Talmud states that there are 48 prerequisites for attainment of Torah (*Ethics of the Fathers* 6:6). Without these prerequisites, one cannot integrate Torah within oneself and one cannot achieve proper spirituality.

Rabbi Mendel of Vitebsk explained that these 48 prerequisites are like receptacles or vessels which can contain Torah. He points out that Torah is often referred to as "the waters of life" (*Bava Kamma* 17a), and it is the nature of water that it adapts to the configuration of the vessel which contains it. I.e., in a round container, the water will take a round form, and in a square container, it will take a square form. Similarly, the 48 character traits are "vessels" in which one can contain Torah, and the quality of Torah one attains therefore depends on the "configuration" of the vessels. If one has developed these traits to a high degree, the quality of Torah one possesses is much greater than if these traits were less developed.

Among the 48 prerequisites of Torah is "to share in the burdens of another." Rabbi Yeruchem Levovitz states that this is even more demanding than the mitzvah to love another person. Sharing in another's burden means achieving so complete an identification with another person that his distress becomes your own.

Sharing another's burden is not an inborn trait. To the contrary, the selfish animalistic trait is the polar opposite of feeling another's distress. Rabbi Yeruchem points to the Talmudic statement that "if there were no fear of the temporal power, one person would swallow another alive" (*Ethics of the Fathers* 3:2), much as a larger fish swallows a smaller fish. A human being is expected to totally reverse this inborn animalistic trait to the point where he identifies with another person sufficiently to share his burden and feel his pain. This is not an easy task, but it is an essential component of spirituality.

The Midrash states that when Moses left Pharaoh's palace and observed the enslavement of his fellow Jews, he put his shoulder under their heavy burdens. Rabbi Yeruchem states that this hardly relieved the suffering of tens of thousands of Jewish slaves, but what it achieved for Moses was that he participated in feeling their anguish, which he could not have achieved by merely observing them.

Yes, we visit the sick and console the bereaved. But can we truly state that we so identify with them that we feel their distress? This is a trait which we must cultivate, and it is a prerequisite for proper integration of Torah and hence for developing spirituality.

The Maggid of Chernobyl, like many other tzaddikim of his time, was dedicated to ransoming Jews from imprisonment by the poritzim (feudal lords). One time the Maggid himself was the victim of a vicious plot and he was imprisoned. He was visited in the prison by a friend, a tzaddik who said, "Why did G–d send the patriarch Abraham on a journey from Mesopotamia to Canaan (Genesis 12:1)? It was because Abraham had excelled in caring for wayfarers, providing them with meals and a place to rest. G–d said to him, 'What you are doing is indeed commendable, but unless you personally experience the exhaustion of a traveler, you cannot understand these people's needs.' G–d therefore sent Abraham on a journey, so that he would have a taste of what it feels like to be a wanderer.

"So it is with you," the tzaddik said to the Maggid. "You have indeed been devoted to ransoming Jews from imprisonment, but you could not do so with total dedication until you experienced the anguish of being in prison yourself. That is why you are here."

This story should help us realize what is expected of us. Even when we do acts of *chesed*, we may not achieve the ultimate of *chesed* unless we can truly participate and share in another's plight.

It is thus evident that *chesed* requires more than acts of benevolence. We must so divest ourselves of egocentricity that we can actually feel the distress of others, and we should be just as diligent in trying to relieve their pain as we would if it were our own. This is not a superhuman feat, because the Torah does not ask us to do the impossible. However, it does require a great deal of self-discipline.

We can best appreciate the overriding importance of *chesed* from the Talmudic statement that *hachnasas orchim* (hospitality to travelers) is a greater merit than being in the immediate Divine presence. This is derived from the scriptural account of the patriarch Abraham, who was in the midst of a Divine revelation when he noticed several wayfarers, and excused himself from G–d's presence in order to greet the travelers and provide them with food and drink (*Shabbos* 127a). Why did the patriarch do so? Because we achieve spirituality by emulating the Divine attributes: "Just as G–d is merciful and gracious, so must you be merciful and gracious" (*Shabbos* 133b). What purpose is there in receiving a Divine revelation if one does not implement the Divine attributes in one's behavior? This would be like receiving a didactic lecture and not following what was being taught. Abraham therefore knew that G–d wished him to attend to the wayfarers rather than to receive the Divine revelation.

Lest we might think that we should extend *chesed* only to those whom we consider deserving of it, the Torah tells us that the patriarch Abraham interceded to save the sinful population of Sodom, people who had descended to the nadir of decadence. One might think that the world might be better off if these morally corrupt people were done away with. The patriarch teaches us that this is not so. We must be considerate of and extend *chesed* to every human being (*Michtav MeEliyahu,* Volume 2, page 181).

As before, we turn to the lives of our Torah personages for practical guidance.

The Talmud says that *gemilas chasadim* (acts of kindness) is greater than *tzedakah* (*Succah* 49b), because *tzedakah* is done with one's belongings, whereas acts of kindness are done with one's person. How far can a person go in giving of oneself?

A chassid of Rabbi Shneur Zalman, who was a poor *melamed*, had five grown daughters who were of marriageable age. Rabbi Shneur Zalman asked the *melamed* why none of his daughters was married. "Who would do a shidduch (matrimonial match) with me?" the *melamed* said. "I am nothing but an insignificant *melamed,* and I don't have money for a dowry. No one would be interested in associating with me."

Rabbi Shneur Zalman said, "I will take one of your daughters as a wife for my son, Dov Ber. Since you will be my *mechuten* (my son's in-law), many people will wish to associate with

you." The humble melamed's eldest daughter be-
came the Rebbetzin of the great Mittler Rebbe,
the successor to the founder of the Lubavitch dy-
nasty!

Doing chesed often took priority over other mitzvos,
and our Torah teachers were displeased with people who
were so devoted to their rituals that they were derelict in
chesed.

O *ne Tishah B'Av, a blind man approached*
one of the worshipers and asked the wor-
shiper if he could lead him home. "I cannot leave
now," the man said, "because I have not finished
reciting the lamentations."

The chassidic master, Rabbi Yechezkel of
Kuzmir, overheard the conversation, and prompt-
ly set aside his Book of Lamentations and
escorted the blind man home. He later repri-
manded the worshiper, "Why are you lamenting
the ruin of the Temple, when it is your own per-
sonal ruin that you should lament. If you are not
aware that doing a chesed of leading a blind
man home is more important than reciting the
lamentations, then you yourself are in ruins."

R *abbi Meir Marim was the Rabbi of Kobrin.*
One time he was found in the house of a poor
man who was sick in bed. The Rabbi was
sweeping the floor, and had prepared food and

drink for the sick man. When the townsfolk said that it was not dignified for the Rabbi to be seen sweeping the floor, Rabbi Meir said, "Who is it that has set the standard for what is or is not dignity? People generally accord the Rabbi the honor of performing a marriage ceremony or being the sandek at a bris. As far as I am concerned, it would be a much greater honor if they would give the Rabbi the opportunity to do something for a sick person who needs the help."

It has been asked, inasmuch as we recite a *berachah* prior to the performance of a mitzvah, why is there no *berachah* for the incomparable mitzvah of *tzedakah?* The answer is that recitation of a *berachah* might delay the act of giving *tzedakah,* and even a momentary delay in helping someone should be avoided. Providing immediate help to the needy supersedes the importance of a *berachah.*

Our great *tzaddikim* have taught us how to prioritize, and they have given *chesed* the highest priority.

Subjugating One's Will

Judaism requires that a person set aside his personal will and adopt the Divine will as his own (*Ethics of the Fathers* 2:4). This is clearly beyond the reach of any living thing other than man, hence it is a component of spirituality.

Earlier we noted that a spiritual person must have an ultimate goal in life. It is therefore proper that everything a person does should be directed, in one way or another, toward reaching that goal. This theme is found in all Torah writings, and is based on the verse, "Acknowledge G–d in all your ways" (*Proverbs* 3:7).

One of the foremost texts on spirituality is *Mesillas*

Yesharim (*Path of the Just*). The term for "just" in Hebrew is *yashar*, which means "straight." We may think of the geometric axiom: "The shortest distance between two points is a straight line." A just or righteous person, who is interested in reaching his goal, will follow a straight path, and avoid deviating from it.

The most serious danger confronting the righteous person is that he might misjudge things. As we have noted, our judgment processes are subject to distortion by our desires, as stated by Solomon, "A man's every way is upright in his own eyes" (*Proverbs* 21:2). It is rare that a person intentionally does something which he believes to be wrong. With our uncanny capacity to rationalize, we can justify anything from the slightest transgression to the most vile atrocities. Solomon warns us against this: "Do not rely upon your own understanding" (*Proverbs* 3:5).

The founder of Alcoholics Anonymous characterized the alcoholic as "self-will run riot"; i.e., the person's will knows no bounds. It is an essential step in recovery from alcoholism that one must set aside one's own will, since the latter has proven itself to be destructive. This is equally true for the non-alcoholic who may be just as adamant in doing what he thinks is right and proper, even though it may in fact be destructive. This is why Rabban Gamliel says that a spiritual person must replace his will with the will of G–d (*Ethics of the Fathers* 2:4).

Inasmuch as the human mind is so vulnerable to being influenced by man's physical cravings and ego aspirations, how can one ever be certain that he is indeed on the path of *yashar*? The answer is that a person must dedicate himself to the Divine will with all the sincerity he can muster, and from there on G–d will take over. "Turn your deeds towards G–d, and your thoughts will be set aright" (*Proverbs* 16:3), and, "Acknowledge G–d in all your ways, and He will smooth your paths" (ibid. 3:6). In other words, if a person sincerely wishes to be *yashar*, at whatever cost to his personal comfort, then G–d will help him be *yashar*.

The Book of *Proverbs* can serve as an excellent text on spirituality. Solomon's observations some 3,000 years ago are as relevant today as the day they were said.

It is a formidable challenge to live a spiritual life when one is in the midst of a society which is anything but spiritual. Our modern world is hedonistic to the extreme, and the moral underpinnings of spirituality have been all but destroyed. Instead of accepting the word of G–d as the unfaltering beacon for leading a straight (*yashar*) life, modern society turns to the man-made laws of legislatures and courts, laws which are intended to appease the public rather than to enforce morality. Just several decades ago, abortion was a crime almost equal to murder. Today it is the natural right of every woman, and must be financed by our taxes. Narcotics threaten to destroy the brains of our youth, and what is a proposed solution? Legalize drugs! People will decide what is right and what is wrong, and according to their viewpoint, G–d help those who believe in an absolute, unchangeable code of morals and ethics. Solomon states it so clearly, "People of violence hate one who has moral integrity, and under the guise of propriety seek to destroy him" (ibid. 29:10).

The spiritual life is not an easy one, and a person is repeatedly confronted by temptations to do things that would divert him from the straight path to his ultimate goal. Committing oneself to a lifelong adherence to spirituality may be overwhelming. Yet, Moses assures us that it is not at all difficult. To the contrary, "It is very close to you — in your mouth and in your heart — to do it" (*Deuteronomy* 30:14). How can it be so easy if we are to struggle against temptation all our life?

The answer is simple. *Do not undertake a lifetime of struggle.* That may seem so formidable that one may give up the battle. Rather, deal today only with today's challenges. Inasmuch as there is nothing you can do today about tomorrow's temptations, leave that struggle for tomorrow, and do not even consider it today. The ability to cope with today's challenges are well within our capacity.

The Torah repeatedly teaches us to take one day at a time. In describing the patriarch Abraham, the Torah says, "He (Abraham) came along *in days*" (*Genesis* 24:1). In his last message to the Israelites (*Deuteronomy* 29:9- 30:20), Moses repeatedly uses the term "this day," and following the verse (ibid. 30:14) which states that the spiritual life is not difficult, Moses says "See, I put before you *this day* life and good, death and evil." How much clearer could he have put it, that the choice between right and wrong, life and death, is one that should be made only for today, and tomorrow's choice should be left for tomorrow.

Solomon reiterates this point when he says: "Reverence of G–d will increase *days*, while the *years* of the wicked will be shortened" (*Proverbs* 10:27), upon which Rabbi Samson Raphael Hirsch comments, "The G–d-fearing man lives in terms of days, and the lawless one in terms of years." Living in terms of years instead of days may cause one to reject the laws of the Torah because they appear to be too great a challenge. And finally, David says, "Blessed is G–d, day by day. He burdens us, the G–d of our salvation" (*Psalms* 68:20).

The spiritual person is thus *yashar*, directing himself day by day toward his ultimate goal, and trusting that by committing himself to the Divine will, he will merit being led by G–d along the path of righteousness.

Simchah

I f *simchah* means only gladness, particularly the gladness of contentment as when all one's needs have been met, then man is not unique in this respect. A cat which has eaten to satiety may curl up in a warm place, and is apparently quite satisfied with both itself and the world. We may even assume that the cat is happy. But *simchah* as it appears in Judaism is much more than this, and in its full meaning is indeed unique to man, hence it is a component of spirituality.

Even the joy of a happy occasion, such as a wedding or *bar mitzvah,* while certainly unique to humans, is not yet the full concept of *simchah.* This is evident from the statement of Rambam that "the *simchah* in doing a mitzvah is a great *avodah* (service of G–d) (*Laws of Lulav* 5:15). The word *avodah* connotes work and effort, which means that the *simchah* of doing a mitzvah is not a spontaneous emotion such as that experienced on a happy occasion. Furthermore, it is obvious that we often do mitzvos without experiencing a sense of elation. The *simchah* of doing a mitzvah is something that we must strive for and make great effort to achieve. Indeed, dereliction in achieving *simchah* upon performance of mitzvos is considered a grave transgression, as is evident from the harsh punishments that will accrue "because you did not worship G–d with *simchah* (*Deuteronomy* 28:47).

The degree of *simchah* one has upon performing a mitzvah may well be a measure of his spirituality, since it indicates his love for G–d and his realization that by doing mitzvos he is fulfilling his mission in life and accomplishing his ultimate goal, that for which he was created.

It is a common experience that when a person is striving to accomplish something of great importance and succeeds in his endeavors, he feels elated, sometimes to the point where he cannot contain his joy and expresses it in song or dance. I recall an incident where a yeshivah wished to enlarge its building due to overcrowding, and some of the neighbors protested the expansion. People tried to get the neighbors to withdraw their objection, but to no avail. Several hearings of the zoning board failed to produce results, and the feeling was that the board was stacked with people who were not sympathetic to the yeshivah. At the last hearing the attitude was one of despair, when miraculously the board voted to permit the expansion. A shout of cheer went up, and several of the yeshivah friends held hands and danced right in the zoning-board conference room! When a sought-for goal is achieved, and especially when it is of great importance, the elation may be boundless.

How much do we value mitzvos? Imagine a person taking a valuable item to a dealer for an appraisal. "How much would you give me for it?" he asks. The dealer quotes a figure, whereupon the person says, "Thank you," and leaves. "Aren't you interested in selling it?" the dealer asks. "No," the person answers, "I just wanted to know how much it is worth."

How much we value a mitzvah is indicated by how much time and effort (and even money) we are willing to put into it. And if we truly value it, we will rejoice in doing it.

The Gaon of Vilna states that the opportunity to do a mitzvah is a Divine gift. Think of how you would feel if you received a valuable gift from a king, personally autographed for you. Why, we even place value on books or other items that bear the signature of an important personality! Now consider that G–d wishes to show His love for you. You might think He would allow you to win the sweepstakes, but G–d knows that money has only a transient value, and not infrequently we see riches generating more harm than good. G–d gives you something of incalculable value: the opportunity to do a mitzvah.

Two people may have radically different reactions upon finding an uncut diamond. One person has no concept of its value, because it does not glitter and looks no different than a piece of broken glass. In all likelihood he will throw it away because he sees it as worthless. The other person is a *mayven* on uncut diamonds, and realizes that he has found something that is worth many thousands of dollars, and he is euphoric with his good luck.

You come into *shul* and you see a notice posted about the need for funds for a destitute family, or for enabling someone to have a lifesaving surgical procedure. You have the opportunity to do the mitzvah of *tzedakah*, something which cannot be measured in dollars. G–d has just shown you how much He loves you by giving you a gift: the opportunity to do a mitzvah! Why is it that we are not elated when this occurs? Why do we not break out in song and dance? You may say because you don't want people to think you are crazy. What if you saw that the lottery numbers that are displayed in the window are those on your ticket, and you are an instant millionaire. Would you restrain your expression of joy because of what people might think?

If we will be honest with ourselves, we will realize how far we are from appreciating the value of a mitzvah.

I t is related that in his last moments of life the Gaon of Vilna wept. Aware that the Gaon knew full well the bliss that would be his in Gan Eden, the people around him were bewildered by his crying. Noticing their perplexity, the Gaon said, "How can I not cry when I am leaving a world where for just a few cents one can acquire an invaluable mitzvah?"

True, the bliss of *Gan Eden* is beyond our comprehension, but the Talmud says that "just a single moment of *teshuvah* and good deeds is worth more than all of *Gan Eden*" (*Ethics of the Fathers* 4:17).

We can see why Torah places so great an emphasis on *simchah shel mitzvah*. How much we rejoice with a mitzvah indicates how much we understand its worth. If we would realize that each mitzvah we do brings us ever closer to G–d, we would feel like someone who has been separated from his beloved and is now going to be reunited. Every step that brings him closer increases his joy.

The *simchah* in the performance of a mitzvah is extremely important. It is traditional to have a *seudas mitzvah* (a festive meal associated with a *mitzvah*), especially on occasions such as a *bris* (circumcision), *pidyon haben* (redemption of the firstborn son), completion of a volume of the Talmud, etc.

One of the chassidic masters explained that when the angel Michael pleads for Israel, he cites the abundance of mitzvos which Jews do. Satan then argues that the Jews are not worthy of Divine salvation, because they do as many sins as they do mitzvos. The angel Michael then rebuts Satan saying, "Even if that were true, have you ever seen a Jew make a festive meal to celebrate a sin? It is only when they do mitzvos that they celebrate, which indicates that if they do sin, it is only because they have fallen victim to temptation, but what they celebrate testifies to what they really value, and it is only mitzvos that they hold dear."

It is therefore important that we celebrate mitzvos with *simchah*, because that is our defense against the Accuser.

Without *simchah*, a mitzvah is incomplete, This concept is contained in a comment by the Netziv, in his explanation as to why the prophet Samuel expressed his concern about the Divine assignment to anoint David as the next king, because he feared that King Saul might become aware of this and kill him. The Netziv states that although the Talmud says that a person should not place his life in jeopardy with the expectation that he will be saved by a miracle, that applies to the average person, but someone who is totally devoted to G–d and has no personal interest whatever may indeed place himself in danger, and rely on being saved by a miracle. Inasmuch as the prophet Samuel certainly had this degree of selfless devotion to G–d, why did he fear exposing himself to danger?

The Netziv answers that inasmuch as the Divine mission was to anoint David to replace Saul as king, and since Samuel was deeply saddened by Saul's loss of the kingship, he felt that he was *unable to fulfill the Divine mission with simchah,* and this was a descent in his spirituality, as a result of which he was no longer able to rely on a miracle (*Haamek Davar, Exodus 32:26*). Let us digest the full impact of this. The great prophet Samuel, who the Talmud says was equivalent to Moses and Aaron put together, felt he had lost his level of spirituality because he was not able to perform a mitzvah with *simchah.*

King David repeatedly refers to his *simchah* in doing mitzvos, as for example, "I rejoice over Your word like someone who has found a great treasure"(*Psalms* 119:162). The reason for this joy can be found in psalm 63:2: "My soul thirsts for You, my flesh longs for You, in a barren, dry desert, totally devoid of water." It is this intense craving for closeness with G–d that allows the Psalmist to conclude, "The king shall rejoice in G–d" (ibid. 63:12).

King David had every right to be morose. The Midrash tells us that there was a great controversy regarding David's lineage. David's father, Yishai, was descended from Ruth, a Moabite woman. Because the Torah prohibits marrying a Moabite convert, Yishai was concerned that he was not permitted to continue in his marriage to a woman of Jewish descent. The Talmud presents the Oral Law interpretation, that this prohibition applies only to *male* Moabites, hence Ruth's marriage to a Jewish man was permissible. However, Yishai was not convinced of this, and separated from his wife, but did not actually divorce her.

Yishai then emancipated one of his maidservants — who thereby became a full-fledged convert to Judaism — with the intention of marrying her. Inasmuch as a Moabite descendant may marry a convert to Judaism, this was acceptable.

Yishai's estranged wife arranged with the maidservant to allow her to take the maidservant's place on the wedding night, and it was then that she conceived David. Yishai was unaware of this ruse, and when his estranged wife was discovered to be with child, he assumed that she had had an adulterous relationship. When David was born, he was therefore considered to be a *mamzer* (illegitimate). Indeed, there were those who wished to execute both David and his mother!

David remained an outcast in Yishai's household until age 28. It was only when the prophet Samuel was instructed by G–d to anoint David as the future king of Israel (*I Samuel* 16:1-13) that the Divine revelation was transmitted to Yishai that David was indeed his legitimate son. Thus, from birth until age 28, David was degraded and rejected, hardly a formative period conducive to mature happiness.

Shortly thereafter, following David's slaying of Goliath, David became a favorite in King Saul's court. However, this pleasant state was short-lived, for Saul turned against David, whom he saw as a threat to his kingship. For the remainder of Saul's reign, David had to flee for his life, relentlessly pursued by Saul and his officers.

Following Saul's death, David ascended to the throne, but was harassed by the followers of King Saul as a usurper. Furthermore, he was tormented by some scholars who challenged his suitability for the kingship because of his Moabite ancestry. The revered scholar, Doeg, challenged the Oral Law's interpretation of the Biblical proscription against marrying Moabite converts as applying only to males, and the elder statesman, Ahitophel, who had been David's bosom friend and mentor, turned against him and became his sworn enemy.

David's son, Absalom, led a bitter revolt against his father, driving him out of the country. The quashing of the rebellion came at a terrible cost to David, as the father of the rebellious son grieved over his child's death. David suffered the anguish of shame because of an incestuous relationship among his children, which resulted in the death of another son. He deeply regretted his behavior with Bathsheba, and for 13 years was bedridden with excruciating pain, which he saw and accepted as expiation for his sin. In anguish he cried out, "O, G–d, how many are my enemies; a multitude rise up against me" (*Psalms* 3:2), and again, "Not a single spot of my flesh is intact because of Your wrath" (ibid. 38:4). Indeed, the Midrash states that David did not experience a single day free of distress in all of his 70 years!

If any human being had grounds for wallowing in pity and self-abasement, it was David. But David set an example for us as to how a person can rise above suffering and adversity, as he became a paragon of humility, strength, and honor. Of all the great personalities which the Jewish nation has produced, it is only of David that we declare, "David, King of Israel, lives on forever!" David perpetuated himself unto eternity by pulling himself from the depths of despair to the dazzling heights of ecstasy and dignity.

David demonstrated for us the compatibility of conflicting emotions. Many times we hear his cries of anguish: "I grow weary with my sighs, and soak my bed with tears" (ibid. 6:7), and, "Until when, O G–d, will you forget me? Until when will you conceal Your countenance from me?" (ibid. 134:2). How deep his feelings of distress were is evident from the following verse: "The pangs of death surround me, and the streams of the wicked frighten me" (ibid. 18:5).

Yet, at the same time, and often virtually in the same breath we hear, "I will gladden and rejoice in You and sing unto Your name, the Most High" (ibid. 9:3). "Therefore my heart rejoices and my glory is glad, even my flesh rests securely" (ibid. 16:9). "Gladden the heart of Your servant, because to You, O G–d, I lift my soul" (ibid. 87:4).

David's humility is legendary. "I am but a worm, and not even a man" (ibid. 22:7). "I am alone and destitute" (ibid. 25:16). "I am so lowly and suffering, only Your salvation can lift me" (ibid. 69:30). "I am lowly and downtrodden, and my heart is empty within me" (ibid. 109:22). But these feelings did not interfere with his sense of greatness. "G–d said to me, 'You are my child ... ask of Me and I will make nations your inheritance" (ibid. 2:7). "G–d rewards me for my righteousness ... for I have observed the ways of G–d" (ibid. 18:21-22). "Protect me, for I am pious" (ibid. 86:2). And in his *magnum opus*, psalm 119, David boldly proclaims his constant devotion to G–d and to His Torah.

David is the *baal teshuvah*, the penitent who bewails his sins. "My sins reach over my head, they weigh upon me like the heaviest burden" (ibid. 38:5). "For I know my sins, and my transgressions are ever before me" (ibid. 51:15). Yet, David is confident that he will be forgiven. "Return to me the joy of Your salvation, and I shall teach sinners Your ways" (ibid. 51:13). "Rest, my soul, because G–d has been gracious to you" (ibid. 116:6).

David had a sense of self-esteem. He composed the immortal psalms because he knew he had the capability. He sang to G–d of the wonders of Creation and of the beauty of the world in the majestic and incomparable psalm 104. He asked of G–d, "May the recitation of my psalms be as worthy in Your eyes as the study of the most intricate and profound portions of the Torah" (*Shocher Tov, Psalms* 59). David had a most personal relationship with G–d, and yearned for even more closeness. "My G–d, I search for You, I thirst for You like a parched throat in the dry desert" (*Psalms* 63:2).

David exemplifies true spirituality, all that is beautiful in man, both in his humanity and his divinity. The Midrash tells us that Adam, who lived for 930 years, was originally destined to live 1,000 years, but when he saw in his prophetic vision that David was destined to die at birth, he donated 70 years of his allotted life span to David.

The relationship of Adam and David is not one of chance. David is the culmination of the Divine intent expressed to Adam, "Let *us* make man." David, the social outcast, who had no peace from enemies within and without, rose to greatness, and sang to G–d with joy: "You have turned my grief into a dance. You have loosened my sackcloth and girded me with joy" (ibid. 30:12). David took the enormous potential with which he was endowed and developed it to the fullest. He indeed became the ideal spiritual man that G–d wished to create.

We can appreciate how intense the elation of being close to G–d was for David, since it brought such great *simchah* to a person who was tormented throughout his entire life, and did not have one day free of suffering.

Although a spiritual person avoids indulgence in physical pleasures, it is important that he supply the body with its needs, which may include pleasure. Rabbeinu Yonah points out that when one denies himself the basic pleasures of life, this may impede spiritual growth (*Shaarei Teshuvah* 2:9). We may understand this with a parable by the Baal Shem Tov.

A young prince was sent into exile for behaving in a manner unbecoming to his station. After a long, wretched period in exile, he received word that he had been granted amnesty and could return to the royal court. His joy was boundless, and he felt he had to express his exultation by dancing. However, he knew that people would think him to be crazy if he did so. He therefore went to an inn and had all the guests served food and drink, to the point where they became giddy and began to dance. The prince joined them and danced along with them. However, their reasons for dancing were radically different. The other people were dancing because they were intoxicated with wine, whereas the prince was dancing because he was going to return to his father's palace.

The Baal Shem Tov explained that the *neshamah* wishes to rejoice in study of Torah, prayer, and performance of mitzvos. However, it is housed within a physical body, and if the body is discontented, it will inhibit the *neshamah's* expression of joy. We therefore give the body adequate food and drink so that it is content and happy, and will not stand in the way of the *neshamah's* happiness. We must be careful, however, not to indulge in physical pleasures, because then the body over-whelms the *neshamah*. Let us remember that the body is the animal component of our being, and while it can not be neglected, it cannot be permitted to become the dominant component.

Spiritual growth may also be impeded if a person feels deprived. There are always people who have more than we do: nicer clothes, better homes, more luxurious cars, etc. Even if one is not frankly greedy, one may be unhappy that he cannot enjoy the goods of the world the way others can, (or at least seem to). It is therefore essential that we have another variety of *simchah*, i.e., to adopt the value system which teach-es us, "Who is a wealthy person? One who is content with his lot" (*Ethics of the Fathers* 4:1). If you find this difficult, please accept my clinical observations. In 35 years of psychiatric practice, I have dealt with people in all walks of life. I have had multimillionaire patients who drowned their misery in alcohol or spent hun-dreds of thousands of dollars poisoning themselves with cocaine in an attempt to relieve their unhappi-ness, and I have had poverty level patients who were happy.

At this point I must confess that I received a *mussar* lesson from one of my patients.

I had just acquired a new automobile, with air-conditioning, full power, and cruise control. I was disappointed to find that the cruise control was faulty, and that it would deviate from the speed at which I set it. In order to get it to func-tion properly, I would have to take the car to the *dealer, and this was a major inconvenience. I grumbled as I drove to the office that day.*

The first patient I saw was a woman who was recovering from alcoholism and was now 10 months sober. She was euphoric about her sobriety and about her accomplishments. She had found a job, albeit at minimum wage, and since her child entered first grade and was at school all day, she was able to work enough hours to afford a better apartment. In a few months she would be able to save enough to have her car repaired.

"What is wrong with your car?" I asked.

"It has no reverse gear," she answered.

"How can you drive without a reverse?" I asked.

"Well, you just have to think ahead. You have to park so that you don't have to back up to get out. But I have to remember that there are some people who don't have a car at all," she said.

I felt chastised and humbled. Here was a person who was happy that she has a car even though it lacked a reverse gear, and I was grumbling because my new car, fully loaded, had an inaccurate cruise control. I realized that I was an ingrate.

I must digress here to tell you something else about this patient. She subsequently developed cancer and underwent surgery and a course of chemotherapy, with all its side effects, including total loss of hair. This woman took pictures of herself in this state, and when her hair grew back thick and lovely, she would visit the hospital and show her picture to cancer patients who were to undergo chemotherapy, to reassure them that not only would they recover from cancer but they would also have full return of their hair.

I believe that these traits are related. Only a person who could be happy with a car that lacked a reverse gear could take pictures of herself while bald, and encourage other patients by sharing her recovery with them. If you think of it, you will realize that taking those pictures while she was bald indicates that she had strong faith that she was going to recover and would be able to put the pictures to use. We thus have a person who is content with whatever she has and is grateful for it, who has trust that she will recover from a life-threatening disease, and who takes time from her day to elevate the spirits of others.

The presence of these traits in one person is not a coincidence, and teaches something about spirituality. Good traits and bad traits generally cannot coexist, at least not for long. It is much like the person who replaces a worn-out living-room chair with a new one. The old couch, which was previously tolerable, now clashes with the new chair, and must be replaced. The new furniture is in stark contrast with the rather shabby carpet, which gives way to a new carpet. But now the drapes are out of "sync" and must be replaced. The decor is incompatible with the wallpaper, and so the latter is replaced. The room is now extremely attractive, and its radically different appearance is the result of replacing a single chair. There may not have been any intent to redo the whole room, but this development was inevitable.

It is much the same with character traits. Good traits are incompatible with bad traits, and once a salutary change is made in one trait, the person will experience an internal conflict which can be resolved only by regressing to the bad trait or progressing to other good traits, and the person who seeks spiritual growth will do the latter. This is contained in the Talmudic statement, "One who begins to improve himself is supported in his effort" (*Shabbos* 104a). If one makes a start at spirituality and has a sincere desire to progress, it will be surprisingly easy.

We have now seen that there are several categories of *simchah*. There is the *simchah* of spontaneous joy on happy occasions, there is the *simchah* which we must cultivate upon performance of mitzvos, and there is the *simchah* of being content with whatever one has.

There is yet another variety of *simchah* which requires a bit of explanation. The Talmud states that a person must praise G–d when bad things happen just as one does for good things. Furthermore, the praise must be given with *simchah* (*Berachos* 60b). Is it realistic for a person to rejoice when bad things happen? We know that the Torah never asks anything of us that is not within our capacity. How, then, can we be expected to praise G–d with *simchah* for adversity?

Rashi (ibid.) provided the answer. In this case, the Talmud does not use the word *simchah* to mean joy, but rather "with a whole heart"; i.e., with trust in the infinite benevolence and wisdom of G–d. One is not expected to be happy with adversity, but rather to accept the Divine judgment with trust in G–d.

*A*s an intern, I assisted in the office of a pediatrician. A mother had brought her baby in for the third dose of immunization, and as soon as the child saw the white-clad doctor, he emitted a shriek of fear. He knew only too well from previous experiences at the hand of this man what was in store for him. Since the nurse was busy elsewhere, the mother restrained the child, who fought and kicked her. As soon as the doctor had administered the shot, the child threw his arms around his mother and held onto her for dear life.

Let us put ourselves in the child's position. "Why is my mother doing this to me? She is the one who loves me and cares for me. Why is she letting this terrible person stab me with a sharp needle and make me hurt for two days?"

Of course, the child has no way of understanding that the pain he is experiencing is a small price to pay for preventing crippling and even fatal diseases, hence he fights the mother and may even momentarily hate her. If the child could understand that his mother is subjecting him to this pain to save him from dreadful diseases, he would be grateful to her.

We are much like the infant in our relationship to G–d. We know that G–d loves us and cares for us, and we cannot understand why he allows bad things to happen to us. Perhaps, if we were able to know the purpose of these distressful happenings, we would be grateful instead of resentful. While the infant's mind cannot reason this way, the mature adult can and should. Logic should tell him that G–d would never allow anything bad to happen if there were not some ultimate good which this will bring about. He should therefore be able to accept adversity with *serenity*, which is what is meant by *simchah* in this context.

> The chassidic master, Rabbi Boruch of Mezhibozh was once reciting the prayer before Kiddush and paused at the words, "I thank you, G–d, for all the kindnesses You have done with me and for all the kindnesses that You will do with me in the future." He reflected, "Why do I have to thank G–d in advance for the kindnesses of the future? Why do I not just wait and thank Him when they occur?"
>
> After a few moments of reflection, Rabbi Boruch said, "Ah! I understand. It may be that when those kindnesses occur, I will not recognize them as such. They may appear in a form that I may feel as distressful, and I may be anything but grateful then." Then Rabbi Boruch began to cry, and said "How tragic it is to be so limited in understanding. Just think! G–d will be doing kindnesses for me and I may not recognize them as such, and may even be resentful when I should be grateful!"

While we certainly wish to be spared any and all adversity, we should be wise enough to exploit it if it should occur. The prophet Micah says, "For after I have fallen I have arisen" (*Micah* 7:8), upon which the Midrash comments, "Had I not fallen I could not have arisen"

(*Shocher Tov, Psalms* 5); i.e., there are some levels of spirituality which a person cannot attain unless he first suffers a setback. The Talmud states, "The level of spirituality reached by a *baal teshuvah* may be unattainable by someone who is a complete *tzaddik*" (*Berachos* 4b). The truly wise person, who according to the Talmud is one who can foresee the future (*Tamid* 32a), may be able to see that in adversity lie the seeds of greatness.

During the lifetime of the Maggid of Mezeritch there were no harsh anti-Semitic decrees, but these were renewed after his death. One of the disciples wondered, inasmuch as the Talmud states that tzaddikim are even greater after their death than during their lifetime, why does the Maggid not intervene to annul the harsh decrees from his lofty position in Gan Eden? The Maggid appeared to him in a dream and said, "When I was on earth, I looked at things through mortal eyes, and when I saw matters that I felt were harmful, I interceded and prayed that they be annulled. But from my vantage point in the Eternal World I can see the ultimate good that will eventuate from these erstwhile adversities, and I cannot intercede to annul something which has an ultimate good."

꒰ ꒱

There is a well-known story of a man who asked the Maggid of Mezeritch to explain how the Talmud can expect a person to express *gratitude for bad things that happen to him. The Maggid referred him to Rabbi Zusia, who happened to be sweeping the floor. When the man posed the question to him, Rabbi Zusia said, "There must be some mistake. I am only the janitor here, and I am not well versed in the Talmud." The man did not accept this and insisted that the Maggid had told him to ask. Rabbi Zusia shrugged and said, "How could I know the answer to that question? Nothing bad has ever happened to me." The man looked at Rabbi Zusia, who was wearing tattered clothes and torn shoes and was obviously racked with pain, and he had the answer to his question.*

You will recall that the infant who fought his mother when she restrained him for the injection promptly threw his arms around her afterward. The painful injection notwithstanding, he knew his mother loved him and that she was the one to whom he must turn for comfort and protection.

The Talmud says that a person is not faulted for being resentful when adversity strikes (*Bava Basra* 16b). Perhaps we are not all expected to have the profound faith and trust that Rabbi Boruch and Rabbi Zusia had, but we should have sufficient faith in G–d's love for us that, like the infant, we turn to G–d for our security.

The Midrash states that G–d never challenges a person with anything that exceeds his ability to cope, (*Shemos Rabbah* 34:1), and one should therefore never feel overwhelmed by adversity.

The Rabbi of Skulen would clandestinely try to protect young men from induction into the Roumanian army, which did not respect religion, and where they would be subject to anti-Semitic persecution. When his actions were uncovered, he was imprisoned and thrown into a dungeon, and his yarmulke was taken from him. The dungeon was cold and wet, and not knowing whether he would ever be released, he felt his days were numbered because he could not survive in these conditions. Deprived of his yarmulke, he pulled his shirt over his head to daven,

When he came to the prayer of Baruch She'amar, he concentrated on the words, "Blessed is G–d Who decrees (gozer) and fulfills (mekayem), Blessed is G–d Who has mercy on the earth, Blessed is G–d Who has mercy on living things, Blessed is G–d Who gives great reward to those who revere Him." At this point he paused and pondered: Inasmuch as the word "gozer" generally refers to harsh decrees, why do we praise G–d for issuing harsh decrees and fulfilling them? Furthermore, since all the other phrases refer to G–d's benevolence, this particular passage seems to be inconsistent with the theme of the prayer.

The Rabbi's first reaction was self-reproach. "How is it that I have been reciting this prayer for so many years, and these questions have never occurred to me before? Have I been praying without the proper kavanah all these years?"

As he continued to reflect on these words, it occurred to the Rabbi that the word "mekayem," which he assumed meant "fulfills," can also mean "supports." The verse then reads, "Blessed is G–d Who supports a person to withstand harsh decrees"; and the praise is that when the Divine wisdom finds it necessary to put a person through distress, G–d gives him the strength to survive the ordeal.

Upon understanding this interpretation, the Rabbi felt relieved. Whatever time he was destined to spend in the dungeon, G–d would give him the strength to survive.

There is a concept in the Talmud of accepting suffering gracefully, and although this may appear beyond our capacity, a clearer understanding of suffering may make this less formidable a demand.

"Pain" and "suffering" are not identical. Let me explain.

It is common practice in medicine to relieve severe pain by administering an injection of morphine. Within minutes the patient feels much better. The pharmacological textbooks state that the action of morphine is much different than that of a local anesthetic. The latter numbs the area by interrupting the pathways that carry the pain sensation to the brain. Morphine does not do this. Morphine allows the pain sensation to reach the brain, but it interrupts those pathways within the brain *that interpret these sensations as distressful.* If the patient is questioned carefully, he will actually report that he stills feels the sensation that he had before, but *that it does not bother him.* This is a medical fact which is taught in pharmacology.

We may have difficulty in understanding this. How can pain not be painful? This seems to be self-contradictory, but the fact is undeniable. *Pain* is a sensation, while *suffering* is the interpretation of this sensation as distressing. Morphine blocks this interpretation. If this still seems incomprehensible, I can personally attest to have treated severe pain with hypnosis, which certainly does not interrupt the conduction of pain sensation to the brain. All that hypnosis can do is essentially what morphine does: block the distressful interpretation, and the patient is relieved of his suffering.

Rabbi Boruch and Rabbi Zusia were able to accomplish with their profound faith and trust in G–d what is accomplished by morphine or by hypnosis.

There is no doubt that animals feel the distress of pain and suffer from it. They have no way of eliminating the "suffering" component of the experience. Man does have this capacity, and while the development of this capacity to the point where one is not distressed by adversity requires a high level of spirituality, it is nevertheless a possibility, and it is therefore a uniquely human feature. To the degree that we perfect this feature, to that degree we are able to have the equanimity which Rashi tells us the Talmud is referring to here as *simchah.*

Having a proper perspective on life may further help the adjustment to adversity.

Let's suppose you have been buying lottery tickets for some time, and voilà! Today's numbers are the ones you had picked! Can this be true? You pinch yourself, and no, you are not dreaming. It has really happened. Still in disbelief, you call to confirm the numbers and recheck your ticket, and it is true. You are a millionaire, the winner of three million dollars! A dream come true.

You rush to the phone to tell your wife the good news, and in your haste you topple a lamp, which hits the floor and breaks into pieces. Too bad! It was an expensive lamp, and you had a great liking for it. But what of it? The loss of the lamp pales into insignificance in light of your windfall wealth.

If the lamp had broken at any other time, it would have been a disaster which you would have taken to heart. You would really have felt bad, and would have brooded over the loss for who knows how long. But today you don't brood, because the elation over your good fortune obscures the loss.

This morning you recited a series of berachos (blessings) thanking G–d for giving you eyesight, for enabling you to get out of bed, for providing you with clothes and shoes, for enabling you to walk, and for giving you strength and energy. You then made a berachah before and after eating, thanking G–d for providing you with food and with the ability to eat it. Indeed, the Talmud says we should thank G–d for every breath we take.

If we really listened to the berachos we recited, then we would not be taking these things for granted. We would realize that there are some people who lack these basic items. Indeed, there are multimillionaires who would gladly part with millions of dollars to have some of the functions we have. Obviously, these functions are gifts from G–d, and they should not be considered any less precious just because we had them yesterday and the day before.

Yes, it is true, you have suffered an adversity which has caused you distress. How deeply would you feel it if you had won millions of dollars today? Well, you have won more than the lottery. You can breathe, see, hear, eat, walk, talk, and care for your bodily needs. In light of this windfall, the disappointment you experienced should shrink in significance. This perspective can enhance *simchah* and enable us to experience at least the variety of *simchah* as defined by Rashi; i.e., to have wholehearted trust in G–d.

Some varieties of *simchah* make life enjoyable, whereas other types of *simchah* may not make life enjoyable in itself, but by making it tolerable, will allow us to experience those events that are merely pleasant as joyful.

Consequences of Behavior

Considering the consequences of one's actions is an important determinant of behavior. The Talmud states "Who is a wise person? One who can foresee the future" (*Tamid* 32a). This does not mean that a wise person is someone who has prophetic powers. That capacity has been attained by only a handful of people throughout history. But everyone has the capacity to achieve wisdom as defined by the Talmud, which is to take into account the possible consequences of one's actions. Lower forms of life cannot contemplate the results of their behavior, hence this is a distinctly human trait.

The Talmud gives an example of consideration of the future, and why this is considered wisdom.

A pious person once came across a man who was clearing his yard, throwing things from it into the street. "Why are you throwing rocks from a property that is not yours into your own?" he asked. The man laughed at this absurd remark and continued doing his task. Years later, his fortunes took a downward turn and he had to sell his property. One day, while walking in the street, he stumbled over one of the rocks he had thrown out years earlier. "How wise that pious man was," he said. "I did not realize that the public thoroughfare would always be mine to use, whereas I might lose my own property" (Bava Kamma 50b).

In the laws of Shabbos, there are many actions which are restricted. Sometimes a person may do something which is in itself permissible, but which has as an inevitable side effect something which is forbidden. Torah law restricts such an act, even though the person really has no intention for the secondary effect. For example, we are not permitted to turn on a light on Shabbos. Now, opening the refrigerator door generally causes a light to go on, hence one may not open this kind of a refrigerator on Shabbos, which is why observant Jews deactivate the refrigerator light for Shabbos. However, a person may say, "But I have no intention of putting on the light, and that is merely an accidental occurrence of my opening the refrigerator." The principle is that if one should be aware of the inevitable consequences of one's action, one cannot claim lack of intent.

Some people who do not appreciate Torah law may scoff at this. "Why make an issue of something as trivial as the refrigerator light?" They are totally missing the point. This is an emphatic statement that **the Torah does not allow a person to divest himself of the responsibility for the consequences of his actions.** If we would only derive the proper teaching from this and apply the lesson of Shabbos to our daily lives and conduct ourselves according to this principle, considering all possible effects of our behavior, how much misery could be avoided!

I wish to digress here, and I know that I may offend some people by asserting that inasmuch as the Torah requires that a person care for his physical health and avoid doing anything that is harmful to the body, I believe that it is therefore *halachically prohibited to smoke cigarettes.* One cannot point to the fact that many Torah luminaries of previous generations were heavy smokers, because the deleterious effects of smoking were not known at the time. In the face of incontrovertible evidence that smoking is damaging to the body in a number of ways, there is no escaping the conclusion that smoking constitutes a violation of Torah law that requires looking after one's health. One must consider the consequences that smoking brings in its wake.

This principle has application in the laws of property damage as well. The Talmud states that a person is liable for any damage he does, even in his sleep (*Bava Kamma* 26a). Thus, if while turning about in bed someone breaks something that had been standing near the bed, he is responsible for the damage, because he should have considered the possibility that this might occur.

What follows next is not at all a digression, but an important application of the responsibility to foresee the future. This is not easy for me to write about, because I know it will distress some people, yet the truth cannot be avoided, even if it is a painful truth.

I do not wish to enter into an moral-ethical-halachic discussion of the issue of disclosure in *shidduchim* (matrimonial matches). This is an issue which is addressed by Torah authorities and whose opinion should be sought. However, there is something which I can discuss from a purely medical-psychiatric aspect.

There are some emotional/psychological problems which are not likely to repeat themselves, and whether a potential bride and groom should reveal these belongs to the moral-ethical-halachic realm which I do not feel qualified to discuss. However, there are some conditions in which there is a significant likelihood of recurrence, and hence disclosure is not only a moral-ethical-halachic issue, but a very practical one. Let me assure you that I am not a callous person, and that my heart bleeds for parents who must deal with the distress of a child with a serious emotional/psychological illness. Let me give two examples of what I mean by a practical rather than only a moral-ethical-halachic concern.

C*ase #1. A young woman of 17 had a severe episode of hyperactivity, which was the manic phase of a bipolar disorder. I urged the family to* have her treated by a psychiatrist, but they were adamant in their refusal, because psychiatric treatment would ruin her chances for a shidduch. The episode lasted several weeks, during which they kept her under tight control at home and fed her Valium. This episode passed as manic episodes generally do. A year later she had a similar episode, and again the parents rejected my advice for treatment. At age 19 she became engaged, and the parents claimed that they had asked a halachic authority who told them that it was not necessary for them to reveal her history. Of course, I have no way of knowing what information they gave to whomever they consulted.

Several weeks before the wedding, the young woman suffered a severe depression, which is the flip side of manic in bipolar disorder. Again, no medical help was sought, but family members tried to prevail on her, and were ultimately able to get her to cooperate to go through with the wedding. The husband had no idea what was happening, and thought that her mood was due to the adjustment to marriage. Shortly thereafter the young woman was expecting, and as her emotional condition deteriorated, the husband informed his parents, who intervened and had her seen by a psychiatrist. At this point the history of the previous episodes emerged, and they were told that since she had three episodes in three years, it was likely that she may have recurrences, and that these could be successfully *treated, but that she would have to remain on medication for the long term. The husband and his parents were enraged that they had been dealt with dishonestly, and considered the marriage contract to be fraudulent. A rabbinical tribunal ruled that she should accept a divorce.*

What was the result of the failure to disclose? The young woman suffered from lack of treatment, the young man was "tainted" as divorced (an unfortunate cultural phenomenon), which would jeopardize subsequent *shidduchim*, and a child was brought into the world under very unfavorable circumstances. I am certain that this young girl's parents felt they were protecting her by not having her treated and not disclosing her condition. But the results were anything but favorable for her. A consideration of the future would have forestalled this painful denouement.

C *ase #2. A 18-year-old man was diagnosed as schizophrenic, and did receive psychiatric treatment. He improved significantly with medication, although he still had some subtle symptoms. A shidduch was arranged with a young woman, who did not detect any abnormality in their single brief meeting, and the history of illness was not disclosed.*

Several months after the marriage the young man stopped taking his medication without doctor's approval, as some patients are apt to do. He then had a severe relapse of schizophrenia, at which time the young woman insisted on a di-

vorce, which she obtained. Had she known that he was being treated for schizophrenia, she might not have agreed to the marriage, or if she did, perhaps she could have been helpful in seeing that he continued his medication.

The young man did not benefit in the least from his parents' well-intended but misguided consideration. When asked why they had not disclosed the problem, they said that it would certainly have ruled out his getting married. But in the end, although he was married, he was soon divorced. Nothing good was accomplished for the young man, while the young woman was the victim of a traumatic experience, and was now "tainted" in her community as a divorcee.

It is therefore important that parents' concern for their children's welfare should not distort their judgment, because this may be to their children's detriment rather than to their benefit. Foreseeing the future and considering the consequences of one's actions does not require prophecy, but only that one be well-informed about the likelihood of what may transpire in the future.

The Talmud says that wisdom is superior to prophecy (*Bava Basra* 12a). While we cannot predict the future, we should be wise enough to implement the uniquely human capacity to consider the consequences of our actions.

11

Intellect

lthough we have taken issue with the definition of man as *Homo sapiens*, it is because this is far too inadequate a term, since, as we have seen, there are many other features that are unique to man and constitute his definition. There is certainly no denying, however, that the human intellect is an important exclusively human character component.

But it is not enough to merely say that intellect itself is a unique human feature. Man has the capacity to *develop* his intellect and increase his knowledge, hence this capacity, too, is a component of the spirit, and in order to be spiritual, man must exercise this capacity to its fullest. To be satisfied with what he already knows and not seek to increase his knowledge is a deficiency in spirituality.

The knowledge accessible to man is enormous, and given the current mushrooming of science and technology, particularly with the incredible retrieval systems of computers and the Internet, there is far more knowledge available to man than he could absorb in several lifetimes. A person must therefore be selective in what knowledge he wishes to acquire. A physician will try to gain as much knowledge as he can about medicine as a whole or in the area of his specialty. An electronics expert will wish to get all the information he can that is relevant to his work. An attempt to learn everything about everything may so overwhelm a person that he will learn nothing at all. Every individual must prioritize and choose whatever is most important for him.

Earlier, we noted several of the goals of life set forth by Torah philosophers. If, indeed, a person adopts a particular ultimate goal, then working toward that goal should be his priority, and consequently he should acquire the maximum knowledge that can help him in pursuit of his goal. Everything else should be secondary and subordinate to the ultimate goal.

Each of the variations of the ultimate goal in Judaism has as a common denominator coming closer to G–d. With this as an ultimate goal, man should invest every bit of time and effort within his capability toward achieving this ultimate goal. Inasmuch as a healthy existence requires shelter, food, clothing, nourishment, and other essentials of life, a person should allot the necessary time and effort toward acquiring those essentials that will promote optimum health, and devote the remainder of his time and effort toward pursuit of his ultimate goal. Most of us would be hard-pressed if we had to be honest with ourselves as to whether this is indeed how we conduct our daily lives.

While it is well within the bounds of spirituality to do whatever is necessary for optimum physical and mental health, which includes adequate rest and entertainment, the term "whatever is necessary" is subject to abuse. For many of us, our actual needs may be but a fraction of what we think we need. Clearly a well-functioning economy car can take care of our transportation needs, yet we may insist on a much more expensive automobile, whose acquisition necessitates devoting more time to make enough money. This may be true as well of our home, clothing, etc.

A spiritual person need not live in abject poverty like Rabbi Zusia, but neither should he need any luxuries. To a spiritual person, anything more than the essentials of life is excessive and unnecessary, and he utilizes the time that would be spent to acquire these excesses to study Torah and do mitzvos. Paradoxically, a spiritual person who makes do with the bare essentials may be much happier than a person who "enjoys" luxuries. As we know, the pursuit of luxury has no end, and just as the desire for wealth may be a bottomless pit, so may be the pursuit of luxury. It is related that a multi-billionaire who was engaged in further increasing his already enormous wealth was asked, "How much money is enough?" To which he responded, "Just a little bit more."

Halachah places great emphasis on using every available moment for study of Torah. Rabbi Shneur Zalman states that in addition to using all available time for Torah, one is also required to use all one's learning capacities in the study of Torah. Thus, a person who has the capacity for a deeper understanding of Torah does not adequately fulfill the mitzvah if he studies Torah only superficially, even though he does use all available time for Torah study.

By the same token, there may be people who, for whatever reason, are limited in their capacity to study Torah. Nevertheless, they can fulfill the mitzvah by supporting Torah scholars, allowing them to devote their time to Torah study. If these people engage in work or business beyond what is necessary for their essential needs in order to be able to support Torah study and education, they are credited with the Torah study that they made possible. Every person thus has an opportunity to maximize himself in Torah study, achieving whatever he can with his given capacities, and/or by enabling others to achieve Torah study.

One should not, however, resign oneself to inadequate study because "I don't have the mind for it." The Talmud relates that Rabbi Preida had a student who was a very slow learner, and Rabbi Preida had to teach him the same lesson 400 times for him to grasp it! Just think of how Rabbi Preida could have put this time to use advancing his own knowledge, yet he felt it was more important to help this student understand something of

Torah. And think also of this student who was so dull that he could not grasp a concept until it was repeated for him 400 times. Both teacher and student had incredible patience, and this could only be because both understood the value of Torah study.

Yes, we are all so busy that we have limited time for Torah study.

> Rabbi Yisrael of Salant, the founder of the mussar movement, was once asked, "Rabbi, I have only 15 minutes a day to study Torah. Is it preferable that I use this time to study Talmud, or should I use it for mussar?"
>
> "For mussar, of course," Rabbi Yisrael said.
>
> "Is mussar really of greater importance than Talmud?" The man asked.
>
> "Not at all," Rabbi Yisrael said, "but if you learn mussar for 15 minutes, you will discover that you can find two hours for Talmud study."

While the number of cells in the human brain is limited, the capacity for better understanding can be expanded. Let us remember that Rabbi Akiva, one of the greatest sages in the Talmud, was illiterate at the age of 40. At an age when most people think that their best years of learning are behind them, Rabbi Akiva began leaning the *aleph beis*, and eventually became the leading scholar of his generation.

Inasmuch as spirituality involves cultivating the intellect, we have infinite room for growth. Regardless of how many times we may have studied a particular portion of Torah, we can always find new meanings in it. We may achieve our maximum physical growth in early adulthood, but our spiritual growth should never come to an end.

There is an apparent paradox in Torah study, and that is that the more knowledge we gain, the more we know how relatively little we know. Indeed, Rambam states that the goal of knowledge is "to know that you know not." The paradoxical character of this disappears when we realize that Torah is Divine, hence it is as infinite as G–d himself. A child's concept of G–d is very simple, but as we mature and develop concepts of eternity and infinity, our concept of G–d progressively expands. So it is with Torah. The more we know of it, the more we realize its infinite character, and the more we realize that what we know is but a fragment of infinity.

Anger

One of the most striking differences between humans and animals is that we have the capacity to control anger. Unfortunately this capacity is too often underutilized.

In his famous letter, Ramban begins by instructing his son to control his anger, and states that this is the key to all desirable traits. Although Ramban later says that humility is the finest of all character traits, he does not advise his son to begin his character improvement by developing humility, but rather by controlling anger. I believe the reason for this is because controlling anger is a matter of managing *behavior*, whereas humility is a matter of developing a feeling. It is much easier to master an action than a sensation.

The Ramban approach supports my discussion of anger in *Lights Along The Way* (*Mesorah Publications, 1995*) where I pointed out that the Hebrew word for anger, *ka'as*, needs to be properly understood, because this single Hebrew word is used to describe three distinct phases of anger.

The first phase of *ka'as* is the *emotion* that is aroused when one is provoked. As a rule, this feeling is not under voluntary control, and with some exceptions, there is little one can do to prevent this feeling. To the contrary, unless one has reached an extremely lofty level of spirituality, failure to feel anger is pathological, just as it is abnormal if one were not to feel pain when pricked with a sharp instrument. There are some people who, for various reasons, have repressed anger, and this can result in troublesome symptoms.

We must understand that *repression* is different than *suppression*. The latter is a conscious process, where a person is aware of a sensation and decides, for whatever reason, to control and suppress it. Repression is an unconscious process, which occurs when an idea or emotion is unacceptable and one wishes to disown it. The idea or emotion is then relegated to the unconscious part of the psyche where it persists and ferments. A repressed emotion is much like a jack-in-the-box which rests on a spring and exerts an upward pressure on the lid. The repressed emotion seeks expression, and one must exert psychic energy to "keep the lid on." At times the upward push on the lid increases, and one must exert additional pressure to keep the lid on tightly, which may result in emotional exhaustion. At other times, when the repressed emotion cannot gain overt expression, it seeks to circumvent the conscience and emerge via sensations and behavior that the conscience or superego will not recognize as being the emotion it wishes to disown, and this behavior may result in neurotic symptoms.

The second phase of ka'as is the *expression* of anger, which can range anywhere from total suppression, to a subdued verbal response, to a loud shout, to a barrage of epithets, to a physical blow, all the way to killing the offender. Whereas the initial feeling upon provocation is not subject to voluntary control, the response thereto is very much subject to control, and a person is fully responsible for how he responds to provocation.

Finally, there is a third phase of ka'as which is the *retention* of the angry feeling. Again, while the initial sensation upon provocation is not subject to voluntary control, one does have the capacity to rid oneself of this sensation, and retaining the anger is a matter of choice.

In order to avoid confusion, it is best to use different terms to refer to these three phases. We will call the initial feeling *anger*, the response thereto *rage* (which may be mild or severe), and the third phase *resentment*. Inasmuch as Ramban advises beginning with mastering behavior rather than a feeling, it is evident that his reference to ka'as is to phase II or rage rather than to the initial feeling. Indeed, when the Talmud condemns ka'as it gives as an example one who breaks objects or tears clothing out of wrath, which is clearly what we are referring to as *rage* (*Shabbos* 105b), and virtually all references in Torah literature to the heinous aspects of *ka'as* are in reference to the manifestation of anger, or *rage*.

Torah literature considers rage to be extremely toxic. "A person who exhibits rage, if he is wise, his wisdom is suspended, and if he is a prophet, his prophetic powers are suspended" (*Pesachim* 66b). Moses, the most spiritual of all humans, was affected by rage. Rabbi Chaim Shmulevitz points out that even justifiable rage is toxic, and cites the above Talmudic source as proof. Moses had every reason to deliver a reprimand, but because he did so with rage, it resulted in a distortion of his judgment. A person may have justifiable cause for putting his hand into a fire to rescue a valuable object, but his hand will be burned nevertheless.

Our own observation corroborates the Talmudic statement that "When one is in rage, all forces of Gehinnom rule over him" (*Nedarim* 22b). We have all seen people who are normally deliberate in judgment make foolish decisions and act in a destructive or self-defeating manner when they lose control of their rage. It is important to be aware that even if their judgment capacity remains intact, the message they wish to convey is nullified by the rage. Most people just turn off their reception when someone screams at them. Solomon was so right: "The words of the wise are said softly and are heard, whereas screaming reigns among fools" (*Ecclesiastes* 9:17).

In addition to rage being morally toxic, our sages also knew that it can cause physical damage. "An angry person is left with nothing but his wrath," upon which

Rashi comments, "He weakens his body but gains nothing" (*Kiddushin* 40b). Angry people die before their time, as is written (*Job* 5:2): "A fool is killed by his anger." Also, "There is nothing that can damage the body as much as anger" (*Tikkun HaMiddos,* Anger, page 85). "The majority of human diseases are the result of anger" (ibid.). Anger impairs one's vision, as is written (*Job* 17:7) "My eyes grew weak with anger." From both moral and health aspects, therefore, rage should be avoided.

Granted, restraining one's natural reaction to respond with rage when provoked may be difficult, but let us remember that failure to do so and acting-out are inborn traits which reduce us to an animal level, something which our pride should not condone.

Some people may claim that it is beyond human capacity to restrain oneself from rage when provoked. Let us remember that it had been known for centuries that it was impossible for a human being to run a mile in less than four minutes. In 1954, Roger Bannister ran the mile in 3:59.4 minutes, and once he made the breakthrough, many runners have duplicated his feat and have done the "impossible." Those who claim that controlling rage is impossible should be aware of the fact that our Torah personalities have made the breakthrough, and that although it may indeed require considerable effort, it is no longer impossible.

Rabbi Menachem Mendel of Lubavitch (*Tzemach Tzedek*) was often provoked by circumstances where it was easy to justify an angry response, and, in fact, where it appeared that to respond in rage to an injustice or a flagrant violation of Torah would be a mitzvah. The Rabbi then reasoned that inasmuch as the Talmud considers rage to be as severe a sin as idolatry, how could a sin possibly become a mitzvah? He concluded that it was necessary for him to study the *halachah* regarding idol worship to see if there was any way this could be permitted for mitzvah purposes, and he would then consult the authoritative works on *halachah*. Of course, since he found that there is never a dispensation for idolatry, he never permitted himself to become enraged, which was equivalent to so great a sin.

Rabbi Chaim Ozer of Vilna was approached by a young man who asked that he write a letter of recommendation for his father, who was applying as a candidate for the rabbinical position in a town. Rabbi Chaim Ozer knew that the man was not qualified for the position, and tried to gently explain to the son that he was unable to write the letter for reasons which he was not free to disclose. The young man became enraged, and began shouting unspeakable insults at the Rabbi, who remained silent. When the young man finished his diatribe, Rabbi Chaim Ozer arose and left the room quietly. A student who observed this asked Rabbi Chaim Ozer how he could restrain himself from responding to such insolence and arrogance. The Rabbi shrugged, "He was just trying to help his father. How could I fault him for that?"

One time Rabbi Chaim Ozer had to sharply rebuke a man for improper conduct. He said to his student, "I am going to speak to him in a manner that will make him think I am angry, so that he should understand the seriousness of his actions. However, I will only be simulating anger, because real anger should never be manifested." The precedent for restraint of anger was set by Hillel.

The Talmud *(Shabbos 30b-31a)* relates that a man wagered that he could provoke the sage to wrath. One Friday afternoon, when Hillel was bathing in preparation for Shabbos, he came to the sage's home and shouted, "Is there a Hillel here? Where is this Hillel?" Hillel quickly dressed and came out to meet the man.

"So, you are Hillel? Then tell me, why do the Babylonians have round heads?"

"A very good question, my child," Hillel said. "It is because the midwives have not been trained well."

An hour later the man reappeared, again exclaiming, "Anyone around here called Hillel?"

Again Hillel emerged, and the man said, "Tell me, why do the Tarmudites have teary eyes?"

"You have been very observant, my child," Hillel said, "and your question is valid. It is because they live in a sandy area and the sand irritates their eyes."

The man continued to return time after time, very close to Shabbos, again audaciously calling for the sage and provoking him with foolish questions which Hillel patiently answered. Finally the man became irate and cursed Hillel, saying "You caused me to lose a wager!" Hillel smiled and said, "There is no wager that is worth losing my temper!"

We need not go back many centuries to find people who had this degree of restraint.

In our own times, there was a tzaddik, Rabbi Shlomo Zalman Auerbach (died 1997), who exhibited similar self-control. Rabbi Yitzchak Freiman, who used to accompany Rabbi Auerbach, once saw the Rabbi remove his tefillin immediately after the morning service, which he was not wont to do. Upon inquiring, the Rabbi said that he was in severe pain and must return home.

As they left the synagogue, a man approached the Rabbi, saying that he had something urgent to ask. Rabbi Freiman told the man that the Rabbi was not feeling well and suggested that he come back at a later time. Rabbi Auerbach said, "No, when a person has a question, you may not procrastinate. What is your question?"

The man explained that because his carpets were very dirty and it was difficult for him to clean them, he rolled them up and set them aside. The woman who lived in the apartment beneath him complained that she could now hear his footsteps and that this irritated her. Was he obligated to replace the carpets and clean them?

Rabbi Freiman was angry with the man for bothering the Rabbi with such a trivial matter when the Rabbi was in pain, but Rabbi Auerbach replied to the man that it was indeed proper that he not cause the neighbor any ag-

*gravation, and that he should restore the carpets.
"Can you recommend a good carpet cleaner?"
the man asked.*

*At this point Rabbi Freiman was about to ex-
plode, but Rabbi Auerbach said, "Go to the
hardware store and ask for this particular carpet
cleaner."*

*As the man left, Rabbi Auerbach said to Rabbi
Freiman, "When a person asks, you must answer
him" (HaTorah HaMisameches, page 313).*

Our great men and women walked in the footsteps of
Hillel, and we must emulate them and follow their demeanor as well as their teachings.

The third phase of *ka'as* is retention of anger, or what
we have termed harboring *resentments*. As we have noted, bearing a grudge makes no sense at all, because the
Torah forbids acting out a grudge in any way, and the offender is thus never affected by the grudge. The only
effect of the grudge is on the bearer, and it can be very
injurious. The quotes we have cited about the toxic effects of *ka'as* on one's health apply to resentments as
well as to rage. Why should the bearer of resentments
punish himself for the offender's behavior? The only
sensible thing is to forgive, and this is why Solomon
says, "*Ka'as* rests in the bosom of a fool" (*Ecclesiastes*
7:9). Solomon is clearly referring here to persistent
anger or resentments, and he calls one who harbors resentments a fool because a wise person would never
punish himself for someone else's misbehavior.

However, logic is not always effective, and if our
emotions defy logic, we may retain resentments even

though they are to our own detriment. How, then, can we rid ourselves of these self-destructive feelings?

We have noted that spirituality is centrifugal, in that it involves looking away from one's own pleasures and comfort and considering other people's needs. Indeed, Rabbi Akiva stated that the all-encompassing rule of Torah is: "Love your fellow man as you do yourself" (*Jerusalem Talmud* 4:9). Although this degree of altruism may appear beyond reach, it is in fact achievable. Moses assured us that fulfillment of Torah is not an impossible task, but to the contrary, "It is very close to you, in your mouth and in your heart, to achieve it" (*Deuteronomy* 30:14).

The word "mitzvah," in addition to meaning "commandment," also means "connection." Mitzvos are the connecting link between man and G–d, and this is the only link that can bridge the otherwise unbridgeable gap between finite man and infinite G–d. Mitzvos are also the connecting link between man and his fellow man. Performance of a mitzvah should therefore bring a person closer to G–d and closer to his fellow man.

Rabbi Yeruchem Levovitz states that Rabbi Akiva's statement that "Love your neighbor" is the *all-encompassing principle* of Torah means that every facet of Torah must relate to this basic concept. Hence, he says, if performance of a mitzvah does not increase one's *ahavas Yisrael*, this indicates that the mitzvah was not performed to the fullest degree.

There is a difference in halachic opinion whether fulfillment of a mitzvah requires *kavanah* (conscious intent), or perhaps one fulfills one's obligation even without *kavanah*. The prevailing opinion is that although absence of *kavanah* is a deficiency, the obligation of doing the mitzvah is generally fulfilled even without *kavanah*. However, although there is technical fulfillment of the mitzvah, the feature of a mitzvah enhancing *ahavas Yisrael* requires *kavanah*. This is why many mitzvos are preceded by the assertion, "I am doing this mitzvah in the name of all of Israel," and when the mitzvah is dedicated in this way, it enhances *ahavas Yisrael*. Unfortunately, too often these introductory words are rattled off without giving much thought to their meaning, which renders the mitzvah devoid of effecting bonding with others.

With some mitzvos, giving more thought to the concepts contained in the mitzvah may help increase one's *ahavas Yisrael*. For example, one technically fulfills the mitzvah of the four species on Succos by holding them together. Torah commentaries elaborate on this mitzvah, and tell us that these four species (the *esrog* [citron], palm branch, myrtle, and willow) are unique, because whereas G–d conducts the world via physical laws and all vegetation is subject to these laws, the four species are under direct supervision of G–d and are not subject to the laws of nature. These four species therefore are symbolic of Divine providence, and should reinforce our belief that G–d attends to every person's needs and provides for them. A sincere conviction of Divine providence should do away with much of the basis for dissension among people, because the knowledge that one will get no more and no less than that which was determined for him by G–d should eliminate the greed, jealousy, and competitiveness which are barriers to bonding with other people.

As we progress in achieving *ahavas Yisrael,* we facilitate divesting ourselves of resentments. It is common experience that although a parent may be provoked to intense anger by a child's misbehavior, this anger is soon dissipated by the intense love for the child. Similarly, as our love for our fellow man increases, our resentments against those who have offended us will diminish. This is why our great Torah personalities, who perfected *ahavas Yisrael,* were, like parents to a child, free of resentments.

Earlier in our discussion of phase I of anger, it was noted that eliciting the sensation of anger upon provocation is virtually a reflex response over which a person "generally" has no voluntary control. "Generally" means that there are some exceptions. What are such exceptions?

Although there is a spontaneous response to provocation that a person may not be able to control, it is possible that he may merit that G–d remove the sensation of anger from him. Prayer can accomplish a great deal, and even those character defects that we may not be able to remove by our own efforts can be removed by G–d.

However, we cannot expect Divine intervention until we have done everything within our own power to curb our anger, which means restraining ourselves from any and all rage reactions, even in the mildest form, and ridding ourselves of all resentments. Then and only then are we justified in asking G–d to remove the natural anger sensation of phase I.

A student of the Chafetz Chaim saw the sage enter the synagogue at midnight and spend some time there. Curious as to what he was doing there alone, the student hid under a bench one night. At midnight the Chafetz Chaim came in, opened the Ark and prayed fervently and tearfully that G–d relieve him of all feelings of anger.

The Chafetz Chaim was never seen to react in anger; i.e., he had mastered phase II, and undoubtedly carried no grudge, having mastered phase III. He was therefore justified in praying to G–d to be relieved of sensations of anger.

Can we aspire to the spirituality of the Chafetz Chaim? Perhaps not, but we can at least identify the goal toward which we aim.

13
Gratitude

C an animals feel and express gratitude? It may seem that domesticated animals, such as dogs, are grateful for what we give them, but their sign of pleasure may be just that; i.e., they are pleased but not really grateful. It is much like the small child who is given a lollipop. He is obviously very pleased with it, but as almost every parent can testify, it may be next to impossible to get him to say, "Thank you." I suggest that true gratitude is a trait that we develop as we mature, and that it is indeed a uniquely human trait.

Small children are not the only ones who may have

difficulty with gratitude. Some adults seem to be very reluctant to express gratitude, and perhaps they may not even feel it. It may surprise us to discover that rather than feeling gratitude, they sometimes may actually develop resentments toward their benefactors.

That some people may react with resentment instead of gratitude can be seen in the account of the Israelites in Egypt. The Torah states that "a new king arose in Egypt who did not know Joseph" (*Exodus* 1:8). How was it possible that within one generation the role of Joseph as savior of Egypt could have been forgotten? The Talmud (*Eruvin* 53a) therefore comments that it was not really a new king who had not known Joseph, but rather the same Pharaoh, who acted *as though he had never known Joseph*. Joseph had not only saved Egypt from being destroyed by famine, but had made it the richest country in the world by gathering the wealth of all the neighboring countries. Furthermore, it was due to Jacob's blessing that the Nile watered the land as never before. How indebted Pharaoh should have been to the Israelites!

It was precisely this sense of indebtedness that turned Pharaoh against the Israelites, and he may have been the first revisionist in history. Joseph never existed! The Israelites are our enemies, and if we are ever attacked they will certainly join forces with the enemy. We must crush them by enslaving them (*Exodus* 1:10). Pharaoh could not tolerate feeling beholden to the Israelites, and what should have generated gratitude resulted instead in resentment, fear, and hostility.

Rabbi Meir Rubman cites the Talmudic statement that a person who does not acknowledge gratitude toward a human benefactor will eventually deny G–d. He cites the example of Pharaoh, who realized that Joseph was endowed with the Divine spirit, and that it was G–d who had given Joseph the wisdom to save Egypt (*Genesis* 41:38), yet he rejected Moses' message from G–d, saying, "Who is G–d that I should obey Him? I do not acknowledge this G–d" (*Exodus* 5:2), a denial of the G–d that saved his country.

Let us therefore be aware that a simple "thank you" brings one closer to G–d.

There is a fascinating passage in the Talmud which states that Moses reprimanded the Israelites as being "ingrates, children of an ingrate." The Talmud states that the first ingrate was Adam, who attempted to defend his sin by saying to G–d, "It was the woman You gave me who made me eat the fruit" (*Genesis* 3:12); hence he was not grateful for the mate that G–d had given him. When were the Israelites ungrateful? When G–d said, "Who would give but that they should always have this reverence for Me" (as they did at Sinai). Moses rebuked the Israelites, "You should have responded to G–d. 'You can give us this gift of reverence.'" The Tosafos commentary explains that the Israelites were reluctant to ask G–d for the gift of reverence because *they did not wish to be beholden to Him* (*Avodah Zarah* 5a).

The Talmud is making a significant psychological observation. If someone is reluctant to feel obligated or beholden for a favor received, he may refuse the favor. The same holds true for one who has already received a favor, who may deny that he received it because he does not wish to feel obligated to his benefactor, and if his denial is not strong enough, he may reinforce it by believing that the benefactor had actually harmed him and was a villain!

Moses rebuked the Israelites because Torah demands that a person acknowledge a favor and be grateful for it. *Halachah* requires that the very first words we utter in the morning be words of thanks to G–d. Our liturgy is replete with expressions of gratitude: in our prayers, in the blessings after meals, and in the various blessings we recite for anything of which we partake. Each morning we express our gratitude to G–d for giving us vision, for enabling us to walk, for giving us clothing, and for giving us strength. We thank Him upon recovering from an illness, or upon arriving safely from a potentially dangerous journey.

One of the effects of praying our liturgy should be that we should become more familiar and comfortable with expressions of gratitude, and this should facilitate our feeling and acknowledging gratitude toward other people as well as toward G–d. It is unfortunate that we take so many things for granted and that especially within the family, we may not express gratitude to our spouses or children, perhaps assuming that they are merely executing their responsibilities toward us.

Reluctance to feel and/or express gratitude may indicate vanity, because a vain person may be grandiose and have delusions of omnipotence, refusing to believe that he may need help from anyone. To a person with low self-esteem, accepting help may confirm his feelings of inadequacy, hence he may deny that he received help. *Halachah* stipulates that a person in need of help must accept it, and has harsh words for someone who denies himself the necessities of life because he is reluctant to accept help.

A vain person may thus deprive himself and his loved ones of legitimate help because he feels this would obligate him. In this case, the capacity to feel and express gratitude could eliminate unnecessary suffering.

Torah literature is replete with the importance of *hakaras hatov* (acknowledging a favor). The weight given to this trait may be seen in the essay of Rabbi Chaim Shmulevitz on this subject (*Sichos Mussar* 5732:32). He refers to the verse in *Exodus* (4:17) where, after being instructed by G–d to go to Egypt and liberate the enslaved Israelites, Moses went first to take leave of his father-in-law, Jethro, who had been hospitable to him when he was a homeless fugitive. Think of it! Several hundred thousand of his brethren are being subjected to unspeakable torture at the hands of the Egyptians, and Moses, although being empowered to bring their suffering to an end, and being specifically commanded by Almighty G–d Himself to liberate them, says that he must first take leave of Jethro! One might think that Moses would not have delayed his mission for even a fraction of a second. But, no! "I must first ask permission from Jethro because he was kind to me." Was this not a blatant defiance of G–d? Why was Moses not reprimanded for this?

Rabbi Shmulevitz points out that Moses had a profound understanding of what G–d expects of man, and he knew that it would indeed please G–d if he showed his gratitude to Jethro by not undertaking his mission without taking leave of him.

The importance given to acknowledgment of a kindness is further evident from the Divine commandment to Moses to have the first three of the 10 plagues inflicted by Aaron rather than by himself, because inasmuch as the river sheltered him when he was an infant, and the sand covered the body of the Egyptian assailant whom he had killed, Moses was not to abuse the water and the sand in the first three plagues. Clearly, it would make no difference to the inanimate water and sand what happened to them, but the point was to set an example that one should be most considerate of any benefactor.

No other mitzvah in the Torah is celebrated with as much pomp as *bikkurim* (the offering of the first-ripened fruits), which is an expression of gratitude to G–d for His bounty. The Talmud states that although a day-worker is not permitted to recite the entire prayer service on his employer's time, he may take time off to greet those who are on the way to bring *bikkurim*. So much does the Torah value an expression of gratitude.

The Torah states that we may not accept male descendants of the Ammonites or Moabites into the Jewish community, because they failed to show their gratitude toward the Israelites when the latter were enroute to Canaan. The patriarch Abraham had placed himself at great risk to save Lot, who was the father of the nations of Ammon and Moab, and their lack of gratitude toward Abraham's descendants could not be forgiven because it indicated a baseness of character. On the other hand, even though the Israelites were so cruelly oppressed by the Egyptians, a third-generation Egyptian convert may join the Jewish community, because we had at one time dwelt in their land, and we must acknowledge their hospitality.

As I have said, the first words we utter in the morning upon arising are *Modeh ani*, I thank You G–d, for restoring my soul and giving me another day of life. The emphasis given to expressing gratitude by making it the first action of the day indicates its overwhelming importance. The spiritual person is a grateful person.

Reverence

Animals do not have a sense of reverence or respect. They do indeed have a hierarchy, and one or more animals may have positions of authority within the herd which may not be challenged, but these are acquired by might. This is equally true of interspecies relationships. A weaker animal will defer to a lion, not because the lion merits reverence, but because of his greater strength. If a dominating animal loses his strength, he concomitantly loses his lofty position as well.

People do indeed respect might and power, but they also have the capacity for reverence; i.e., to respect someone who does not wield any power over them in any way, but whose greater wisdom or refinement of character merits his being revered. This is a uniquely human feature, hence it is a component of spirituality.

In several of my books I have stressed the importance of self-esteem, by which it is meant that a person should have a sense of self-worth and be aware of his character strengths. Self-esteem is not vanity; in fact, it is the polar opposite of vanity. Vanity is actually a desperate attempt at escaping from feelings of unworth, and the vain person seeks approval and acclaim from others to validate him and give him a sense of worthiness.

Showing disdain and disrespect for others is a manifestation of low self-esteem, because by disparaging others, one may try to convince himself that he is superior to them.

The Talmud says: "Who is a respected person? One who shows respect to others" (*Ethics of the Fathers* 4:1). A person who has a healthy self-respect has no need to resort to degrading others in order to prove himself as superior to them. Behaving disrespectfully thus betrays a sense of low self-esteem.

Torah is most explicit in demanding proper reverence. One of the Ten Commandments is that one must respect one's parents (*Exodus* 20:12). There is also a specific mitzvah that one should show respect to the wise and elderly (*Leviticus* 19:32). Indeed, halachic guidelines of respect are most stringent. The Talmud gives an example of Dama ben Nesinah who was sitting with the elders of Rome when his mother, who was mentally deranged, approached him, tore his garment from him, and spat in his face, and he restrained hims⟨ responding disrespectfully.

The authors of the Talmud did not mince any wɔ. concerning disrespect, not only toward parents and elders, but toward every human being. Humiliating someone publicly is considered the gravest of all sins, not only equivalent to murder, but even surpassing it in severity. "One who humiliates his fellow in public — though he may have Torah and many mitzvos to his credit has no share in the World to Come" (*Ethics of the Fathers* 3:15).

One might ask, inasmuch as even a murderer is not denied the heavenly reward that he had earned with his good deeds, why is someone who shames a person publicly dealt with more harshly? "Because," says *Tanna D'bei Eliyahu*, "physical death is a one-time event, whereas public humiliation is a long, drawn-out death. By publicly humiliating a person, he kills him many times." This is echoed by Rabbeinu Yonah who says, "The suffering of public humiliation is greater than that of dying" (*Shaarei Teshuvah* 3:139).

Man was created in the image of G–d (*Genesis* 1:27). Behaving disrespectfully to a human being is essentially a denial of the Divine origin of man (*Tiferes Yisrael, Ethics of the Fathers* 3, note 72). "Referring to someone with a derogatory nickname is a severe sin, even if that person has become accustomed to it. Although other sinners eventually emerge from Gehinnom, one who shames another publicly never emerges from Gehinnom" (*Bava Metzia* 55b). "The reason one who humiliates another is dealt with so harshly is because this is evidence of gross character deficiency, which is not true of someone who commits even a grave sin because he could not withstand temptation" (*Nachal Kedumim, Kiddushin*).

In prayer we strive to bring ourselves ever closer to G–d, and the expression of our devotion reaches its zenith in the reading of the *Shema*. *Halachah* states that during recitation of the *Shema*, one is not allowed to interrupt in any way, even to indicate something by signaling, and even if it is for the purpose of a mitzvah. Yet, one is permitted to respond if greeted by another person [if that person would be greatly offended]. Why? Because showing respect to another person is equivalent to showing respect to G–d. The Talmud says that on Judgment Day one will be asked, "Did you relate respectfully to G–d?" And, "Did you relate respectfully to your fellow man?" Both are given equal value (*Tikkun HaMiddos*, Be Cautious in the Respect of your Fellow Man, page 85).

We hardly find as much emphasis on any other *halachah* as on respect for another person. "Do not engage another person in discussion of Torah unless you know he is capable of holding his own, lest you cause him embarrassment" (*Sefer Chassidim* §312). The Talmud states that when a person would bring a sin offering to the Temple, it was prepared in the same area as other offerings, so that the person would not be identified as a sinner. The Midrash states that because Moses referred to the Israelites as "a brood of sinful people" (*Numbers* 32:14), his grandson became the priest of an idol (*Yalkut Reuveni, Mattos*). Think of it! Moses, whose every move was dedicated to the glory of G–d, and who reprimanded the Israelites for straying from G–d's ways, the great Moses was punished harshly for not addressing the Israelites with proper respect (*Tikkun HaMiddos*, ibid., page 66). And finally, although the Talmud refers to the sin of humiliating someone publicly, the Chafetz Chaim states that this applies equally to humiliating someone in private (ibid., page 125).

As much as we can learn from the precious teachings of our great Torah personalities, we can learn even more from the way they lived, whereby they implemented their teachings in their behavior.

A s a young man, Rabbi Akiva Eiger visited his future father-in-law, and some of the town's leading Talmudists came to see him, since his reputation as a Talmudic genius has preceded him. To their astonishment, Rabbi Akiva Eiger hardly entered into their discussions, and it was their impression that he was a very shallow scholar at best. His father-in-law-to-be felt that he had been deceived and wished to break the engagement and send him home. Rabbi Akiva Eiger persuaded him to allow him to remain for a week. After the week passed, Rabbi Akiva Eiger summoned the town's scholars and began to expound on Talmud in a manner that stunned them. His future father-in-law asked him why he had kept his silence so long and allowed people to think him to be ignorant. Rabbi Akiva Eiger explained, "There was a young man in town who was visiting his future in-laws, and he had been hailed as a great scholar. I knew that if I were to enter into Talmudic discussions, I would upstage this young man and he would feel slighted. I therefore waited until he left town before allowing myself to expound on the Talmud."

Just how dear the respect of another person should be can be seen from this anecdote of Rabbi Issar Zalman Meltzer. Several of his students were at his home when one looked out the window, and it appeared to him that the Rabbi of Brisk was approaching the house. The student alerted Rabbi Issar Zalman, who promptly put on his Shabbos kaftan, and ran down the stairs to greet the tzaddik, only to discover that the student had been mistaken. It was not the Rabbi of Brisk.

Nevertheless, Rabbi Issar Zalman behaved as though this person had indeed been the Rabbi of Brisk. He sat him at the head of the table and asked, "May I serve you something? Perhaps something to drink?" The man was bewildered at this unusual reception and said, "Please, Rabbi, don't exert yourself in the least ... I have come to ask a favor of you. I am compelled to go to raise funds to marry off my daughter, and I wonder if you would be kind enough to give me a letter of recommendation."

"Of course," Rabbi Issar Zalman said, "with great pleasure." And he promptly wrote the desired letter, gave it to the man, and escorted him to the street, just as if he had been the Rabbi of Brisk.

When the students asked the Rabbi why he had given so much honor to this person, Rabbi Issar Zalman responded, "The truth is that we should behave with the utmost reverence toward every person, just as the patriarch Abraham did toward the three visitors whom he thought to be Arabs. Unfortunately, we are derelict in this, and we discriminate among people according to their social status. But when Divine providence engineered it so that I had prepared to show great respect for the illustrious tzaddik of Brisk, how could I reject the opportunity to show the respect that we should indeed have for everyone, even for a simple person?"

The Midrash states that G–d said to the heavenly angels, "Look at the marvelous creature I have created." He could have said this (and perhaps did) about Rabbi Akiva Eiger and Rabbi Issar Zalman Meltzer. This is an excellent example of spirituality at its best, of a kind of behavior which is far, far beyond the capacity of any living thing other than man.

We teach our children primarily by modeling for them, and Rabbi Shlomo Eiger was a true son of his father, in whose footsteps he followed. In his will, Rabbi Shlomo Eiger admonishes his son, "I have noted that when members of your household talk loudly, you say something like 'keep quiet' to them. Please get out of the habit of silencing people, because you might, as a matter of habit, make a similar remark to someone who will feel offended by this. It is important that you break a habit that may embarrass someone."

Rabbi Yosef Dov Soloveitchik was once involved in a lively Talmudic discussion with another Torah scholar, Rabbi Ezriel of Berlin, and when the latter began posing a particular argument, Rabbi Yosef Dov interrupted, saying "Yes, I am aware of that opinion." He later regretted his rudeness and wrote a letter of apology to Rabbi Ezriel, begging forgiveness for his lack of respect.

Rabbi Yehoshua Leib Diskin was giving a Torah lecture to a group of his students, when he was served a glass of tea. After he drank the tea, the Rabbi's wife noted that the student who had served the tea had used the salt shaker instead of the sugar bowl, and upon tasting the few drops of tea that remained in the glass, she found them to be very salty.

"Why didn't you send back the tea?" she asked the Rabbi. "What! And embarrass the student who served it?" the Rabbi responded. "But you are not allowed to have any salt," she protested. The Rabbi responded, "The Torah says that it is better for a person to throw himself into a fiery furnace rather than to cause someone to be humiliated."

How sensitive must one be about protecting another person's honor? The Chafetz Chaim has been our teacher par excellence via his voluminous halachic works, but his behavior teaches us even more.

The Chafetz Chaim and Rabbi Moshe Londinsky, who was the head of the yeshivah in Radin, once traveled together, and, upon alighting from the train, the Chafetz Chaim refused to allow Rabbi Moshe, who was many years his junior, to carry his bags for him. Some people who greeted them assumed that Rabbi Moshe was the sage's aide, and reprimanded him, "How do you allow your master to carry his own bags?" The Chafetz Chaim was horrified. "Take heed how you address Rabbi Moshe," he said. "He is a great Torah scholar." The Chafetz Chaim then apologized to Rabbi Moshe and begged his forgiveness, because he felt he had indirectly been the cause of others offending him.

The level of one's character may be best evaluated by how one relates to others. A person who has reverence for G–d and respect for other people is indeed spiritual.

15

Rejoicing with Others

I t is clear that a major difference between animals and humans is that all animal drives are centripetal; i.e., they are all directed to self-gratification. A human being can have centrifugal drives, rejoicing when others are gratified.

There is reason to believe that animals are capable of envy, or at least something akin to it. Animals will fight over food, and the loser will walk away with what appears to be disappointment, probably resentful that the other animal has the food rather than him. This is about as close to envy as one can get. There is nothing to indicate, however, that an animal can be happy when other animals attain something. Taking pleasure in another's success is a singularly human feature, hence, it too is a component of spirituality. We thus have polar opposites: Being envious of someone else is an animal trait, whereas rejoicing with another person's happiness is a human trait. We ascend in spirituality when we do the latter, and descend when we are envious.

Envy is not only a reprehensible trait, but is also a futile and distressing feeling which can affect a person both emotionally and physically. The latter was emphatically stated by Solomon, who was obviously aware of the psychosomatic consequences of envy when he said "A kind (lit. soft) heart provides for life, while envy rots one's bones" (*Proverbs* 14:30). The harm of envy is compounded by the fact that it is so futile, because begrudging another person's success gains one nothing.

Envy is virtually identical with coveting that which belongs to others, which is explicitly forbidden by the Tenth Commandment. Envy is not only the antithesis of spirituality in its own right, but also betrays the existence of other major defects, as pointed out by Ibn Ezra.

Ibn Ezra raises the question: How can the Torah forbid one to covet? It is reasonable to expect of a person to be in control of his actions and behavior, which is what all the other commandments require, but how can one control a feeling? If one has a desire for something that another person has, is it reasonable to expect him to quell that desire?

Ibn Ezra provides a valid psychological answer. Suppose a person who is greedy were to be told that a powerful telescope on a satellite detected mountains of gold and diamonds on a star several hundred light years away. (Ibn Ezra did not, of course, use this metaphor in the 12th century.) One could become immensely wealthy by hauling off buckets of gold and jewels. Even though this person hungers for wealth, he would not give this source of riches any serious thought whatever. Why? Because since it is countless trillions of miles distant, it is completely inaccessible and will be so forever. In other words, Ibn Ezra says that a person will not have any desire for something that is totally beyond his reach.

If so, Ibn Ezra continues, why would a person covet someone else's wife or belongings? It can only be because, however remote a possibility, these are not considered totally beyond one's reach. But they would not be at all accessible if a person were absolutely committed to observance of the other commandments: You shall not kill, You shall not steal, You shall not commit adultery, You shall not bear false witness. Therefore, Ibn Ezra reasons, if one has a desire for something that belongs to another person, it means that it is not as completely inaccessible as the gold or diamonds on a distant star, and this can only be because one's commitment to the other commandments is not absolute. Clearly, the latter constitutes a major character defect.

The converse of envy is taking pleasure in another person's success, and being happy that he has the goods in life. You can easily measure this aspect of spirituality in yourself by seeing how you would react if an acquaintance of yours were to receive a major promotion at his job, or if you were truly happy if he were able to buy a new luxury automobile, while you are driving an old, beat-up model.

Parents generally take pleasure in their children's success, even when their children surpass them. The Talmud states, "A person is not envious of his child or of his student" (*Sanhedrin* 105b). The reason for this is that children and students are considered extensions of one's self, and their gain is also the gain of the parent or teacher. If we achieve what Hillel said is the basis of Torah, to love one's neighbor as one's self, this would be akin to the parent/child or teacher/student relationship, and one would partake in another's happiness as if it were one's own.

Judaism teaches that spiritual drives are an expression of the *neshamah* (soul). The Torah states that when G–d created man, He "breathed the breath of life into him" (*Genesis* 2:7), and the *Zohar* points out that when one exhales, he exhales something from within himself. Thus, G–d breathing a breath of life into man means that He put something of Himself into man, and the human spirit is therefore a "part," as it were, of G–d Himself. Since G–d is absolute unity, all *neshamos* are one, hence all humans are one in spirit.

The fact that we are separate individuals is because our physical bodies are distinct. In other words, mankind is one in spirit, but many in body. To the extent that we give priority to the spiritual aspect of our being, to that extent we are united as one. To the extent that we emphasize the physical aspect of our being, to that degree we are separate.

We can now understand why Hillel considered "Love your neighbor" to be the essence of Judaism: because such love is attainable only when we fulfill our spiritual drives. The more we indulge our physical selves, the more we separate from one another. Spirituality and unity are therefore two aspects of the same principle. Complete observance of all Torah tenets, the ethical/moral as well as the ritual, will result in the attainment of spirituality and unity.

Forgiveness

t is inconceivable that animals can forgive. Quite the contrary, legend has it that elephants never forget, and animals of higher intelligence seem to have excellent memories. Dogs will avoid someone who has hurt them in the past, and if sufficiently secure, may attack him. The capacity to forgive an offense is clearly a human feature.

As noted earlier, spirituality can be attained by total observance of Torah, the moral-ethical as well as ritual mitzvos. The Torah prohibits you from taking revenge against someone who has offended you (*Leviticus* 19:18). It goes even one step further, in that if someone who offended you in the past now asks a favor of you, not only may you not take revenge by refusing him, but it is also forbidden to say, "Yes, I will do it for you even though you do not deserve it, after the way you treated me. I am not like you." You must do the favor without referring to his offense against you in the past.

Inasmuch as one cannot act out a grudge in any way, what point is there in hanging onto the resentments? The person who offended you is not going to be affected in any way by your resentments against him, since you cannot act upon them. The only one who will be negatively affected is you, because it is the nature of resentments that they generate all kinds of misery: migraine headaches, stomach ulcers, high blood pressure, and circulatory problems. Ironically, if you retain resentments against someone who offended you, you are harming yourself rather than him! Where is the logic in hurting yourself because someone else offended you? By forgiving the person and divesting yourself of the resentment against him, you are doing yourself the greater favor.

Halachah requires that a person should forgive anyone who offers an apology for his behavior (*Orach Chaim* 606:3). The *mussar* works add that we should forgive anyone who has offended us even if he does not offer an apology, and quotes the Talmud which states that if a person forgives others, he will merit forgiveness for his sins (*Yoma* 23a). The Baal Shem Tov interprets the verse "G–d is your shadow" (*Psalms* 121:5) to mean that just as the shadow mimics a person's moves, so does G–d conduct Himself toward us according to the way we behave toward others. Hence, if we overlook misdeeds others have done to us, G–d will overlook our misdeeds.

Halachah states that Divine forgiveness is effective only for those who believe that G–d forgives, but that if someone says, "Of what purpose is Yom Kippur? My sins will never be forgiven anyway," then he is indeed not forgiven. We must have faith in Divine forgiveness, for the prophet says, "I have erased your sins like a fog that has dispersed" (*Isaiah* 44:22). Just as there is no residue of the fog, so there is no residue of a sin that has been forgiven, and we must be accepting of this.

Not infrequently, we encounter people who have done *teshuvah* for their mistakes, but continue to harbor guilt feelings. Guilt can be constructive, just as physical pain can be constructive. If we had no physical pain, we would not know when to protect ourselves from injury, and we would have no clue when things were going awry with our body. Similarly, guilt can be constructive when the desire to avoid feeling guilty deters us from doing wrong, or when it causes us to take corrective actions for the wrongs we have done. However, once we have done *teshuvah* and have resolved not to repeat our wrongful behavior, hanging onto this guilt no longer serves any constructive purpose, and indeed, it is then destructive, since it can impede our functioning and cause us to become depressed. It is therefore important that we accept Divine forgiveness, and forgive ourselves as well.

It is well to remember that the *yetzer hara* has but one goal: to disable us from performance of mitzvos. How it achieves that goal is irrelevant. The *yetzer hara* is cunning in its tactics, and knows how to attack each individual where he is most vulnerable. Some people can be rather easily seduced to transgress Torah prohibitions. With others, who are dedicated to observance of Torah, and who cannot be seduced to violate Shabbos or eat *tereifah,* the *yetzer hara* tries to disable them by making them feel sinful, unworthy, and undeserving of a close relationship with G–d. It can achieve this under the guise of piety, causing a person to think, "How can I expect G–d to love me and to wish me to be closer to Him when I have been so sinful?" This is a thought which is appropriate before *teshuvah,* and which will stimulate a person to do *teshuvah,* but after *teshuvah,* a person should feel free of the burden of sin, and realize that by doing *teshuvah* he has come very close to G–d. Indeed, according to the Talmud, he may be even more deserving than someone who has never sinned, because he has been able to overcome his proclivity to sin, and has thus exerted himself to do the will of G–d even more than a person who has not yielded to temptation (*Berachos* 34b).

Another reason why a person may have difficulty in accepting forgiveness is because it may be a foreign concept to him. If someone has never been able to forgive others, he may not have any understanding that there can be such a thing. Forgiving others is therefore not only something by which we may merit Divine forgiveness, but also something which can help us accept that we, too, can be forgiven.

P*rior to becoming Rabbi of Berditchev, Rabbi Levi Yitzchak was Rabbi in a town where* *there were a number of people who were hostile toward him, and once when he was out of town, his adversaries placed his wife and children on a wagon used for hauling trash and sent them out of town. Rabbi Levi Yitzchak's colleagues, infuriated by this atrocity, asked Rabbi Zev of Zhitomir to invoke the wrath of G–d on the perpetrators of this outrage. "You have come too late," Rabbi Zev said. "Levi Yitzchak is already standing at the open Ark, praying fervently that no harm befall them."*

Forgiveness is an application of the fundamental principle of Judaism, "Love your neighbor as yourself" (*Leviticus* 19:18). If we have offended someone, we would certainly wish to be forgiven, hence we should extend this courtesy to those who have offended us.

Just as it is important to grant forgiveness, it is equally important to ask for it. Let us note that animals are incapable of asking for forgiveness just as they cannot grant it, hence both of these are uniquely human traits and are therefore spiritual in nature. *Halachah* states that if we have sinned by offending someone, we cannot receive Divine forgiveness until we have asked for forgiveness from that person.

Vain people, who are likely to have a false sense of pride, may feel that it is demeaning to ask for forgiveness, and may find it difficult to admit that they erred. There is a beautiful passage in the Talmud (*Chullin* 60b) which states that at the time of Creation, the sun and moon were equally bright. The moon complained to G–d that there cannot be two luminaries of equal light, saying, "Two kings cannot share one crown." G–d responded by commanding the moon to sharply diminish its brightness.

The Torah states that on Rosh Chodesh, the first day of the lunar month, we are to bring an additional sin offering (*Numbers* 28:15), and the Talmud states that this offering is because G–d wishes to be forgiven for having diminished the light of the moon. If it is not beneath the dignity of G–d to ask for forgiveness, why should a human being consider it demeaning?

Forgiveness is another item which is dependent on self-esteem. A person who is haunted by feelings of inferiority is likely to be reluctant to ask for forgiveness. Almighty G–d is the absolute of all perfection, hence He is also humble. "Wherever you find the greatness of G–d, there you will find His humility" (*Megillah* 31a). As we become more spiritual and emulate the Divine attributes, we become more like G–d, and our self-esteem allows us to be humble. Our sense of worthiness, which is not to be confused with vanity, can enable us to both forgive and to ask for forgiveness.

17 *Truth*

ot all traits that are unique to humans are admirable. For example, people are the only living creatures that can lie. Animals, as far as we can tell, are unable to lie. According to our definition then, the capacity to lie must therefore be a component of the spirit! This should not shock us, since we are told that we have a *yetzer hara,* which is a negative component of the spirit. In this case, being spiritual means *suppressing* this negative capacity rather than implementing it.

We might conjecture, why is it that humans are the only creatures that can lie? Perhaps it is due to the fact that, as we noted earlier, animals come into the world essentially complete, and need to grow only in size and shape. They do not have to change their character. It is the nature of the bear to hibernate for months, and it is the nature of the lion to kill for food. When bears and lions behave this way, they are not indolent nor are they murderers. They are merely exercising their innate nature, and they are true to what they were intended to be. The hibernating bear is very much a bear, and the predator lion is very much a lion. Hence, an animal is a *true being*.

Man is different. As we have pointed out earlier, man is born incomplete, and he must develop himself into the being he was intended to be. In *Let Us Make Man* I offered an explanation for the term used in the Torah for creation of man: "G–d said, let *us* make man" (*Genesis* 1:26). The question is obvious. Whom is G–d including with the term "us," and why is this term used only in regard to creation of man, and not with any other living thing? The answer may be that animals are created complete and need not do anything to become something other than they were created. Man, however, is an incomplete creature, and it was the Divine intention that man work to develop himself into what he was intended to be: a spiritual being. G–d could certainly have created man as a full-fledged spiritual being, but then man would essentially be an angel. It was the Divine wish that there be animals, which are purely physical beings, and angels, which are purely spiritual. The Divine concept of man was that he was to be a being that would be created imperfect and would work toward perfecting himself.

To have created him already spiritual would not have fulfilled the Divine intent. Since man must develop himself into the Divine concept of a physical being that strives for spiritual perfection, G–d elicits man's participation in bringing about the finished product. The "us" thus means man himself, and G–d was essentially saying to man, "I am creating you with the potential and capacities to become what you should be, and you must do the rest." Man, as it were, therefore participates in his own creation. (I was thrilled to subsequently discover that the Baal Shem Tov interpreted this verse the same way.) We can now better understand why the Talmud says that a person who observes the Torah is considered "a partner with G–d in the work of Creation" (*Shabbos* 10a). A partner, indeed, because he shares with G–d in the creation of man

A person is a true man when he strives for spiritual perfection, and only when he does so, because he is then the being that G–d intended. This is in contrast to animals, who are from birth the being that G–d wanted to create. Since animals are true to themselves, they do not lie. When man strives for spiritual perfection, he does not lie, and he is then true man. When he does not strive for spiritual perfection, he is not true man, hence he is capable of lying.

The Torah considers truth to be the sine-qua-non of spirituality. The prophet says, "G–d is truth" (*Jeremiah* 10:10), and since the goal of spirituality, as noted, is to identify with G–d, spiritual man must be true. The pivotal role of truth can be gathered from the fact that there is no other prohibition wherein the Torah requires that a person distance himself from that transgression. The scriptural requirement is that we must not commit prohibited acts, and there are many restrictions of rabbinical origin that act as safeguards to help us avoid transgressing. Falsehood is the only prohibition where Scripture itself requires one to distance himself from it. Whereas the Torah forbids lying (*Leviticus* 19:11), it is not content with this, and adds "Keep a distance from falsehood" (*Exodus* 23:7), which means that one should avoid any behavior that might result in one having to deny doing it. Although G–d has infinite tolerance for sinful people, he cannot countenance someone who lies (*Psalms* 101:7).

The works of *mussar* are replete with condemnation of falsehood. "One who speaks falsely denies the true G–d" (*Shaarei Kedushah*, Rabbi Chaim Vital). "If one lies it is as though he has transgressed *all* the mitzvos (*Midrash Talpios* 35). Chida states: "One who lies excludes himself from the congregation of Israel" (*Lev David* 16). The *Maggid* of Kelm said that a liar is even worse than a thief or a strong-armed robber. A thief works only in stealth, usually under cover of darkness, and the strong-armed robber, who may rob in broad daylight, will do so only with a victim who is weaker than he, and only with an individual. He will not rob a large multitude. A liar, on the other hand, lies both day and night, to both the weak and the strong, to both individuals and the populace in general.

T*he chassidic master, Rabbi Pinchas of Koretz, was absolutely dedicated to truth. He once said, "Nothing in my life was as difficult for me to* achieve as eradicating every trace of falsehood from my being. This took me 13 years of hard work, but I finally arrived at a point where I will not commit even an iota of falsehood."

∽∼

Rabbi Pinchas had as a disciple Rabbi Raphael of Bershad, who reached the zenith of devotion to truth. One of the townspeople was accused of bringing contraband merchandise into the country, and because he was a Jew, he would have been sentenced to a lifetime of exile in Siberia, a punishment which was more than just "cruel and unusual." Rabbi Raphael was told that his name had been submitted to the magistrate as a character witness, and that if he testified for this man, the charges would be dismissed.

Rabbi Raphael was in a quandary because he believed the man to be dishonest, and for him to testify otherwise would be lying, which was abhorrent to him. On the other hand, if he refused to testify, that would indicate that the person was indeed dishonest, and would result in an inhumane punishment which far exceeded the crime. Rabbi Raphael prayed that G–d deliver him from this terrible dilemma. He wept all night, and toward dawn he died, in the midst of his tearful prayers.

∽∼

A disciple of Rabbi Raphael once gave the Rabbi's wife a silver candelabrum. When Rabbi Raphael saw it, he said to his wife, "A silver candelabrum is an unnecessary and excessive luxury." The wife reassured him that it was not really silver but only silver-plated. "What!" the Rabbi exclaimed, "then it is both a luxury and a deception," and he insisted that she dispose of it. Anything that smacked of falsehood was anathema to him.

It is related that Rabbi Raphael learned that one of his children had told a lie. He was crushed, as though his whole life was purposeless if he had brought into the world a person who lied. Rabbi Raphael actually sat shivah (the mourning ritual), which was also observed if one's child rejected Judaism and took on another religion.

There are many accounts of how our Torah luminaries were uncompromising when it came to truth. As far as they were concerned, the sin of lying was virtually in the category of the three cardinal sins of murder, forbidden relationships, and idolatry, for which a person is required to accept martyrdom rather than commit them. Lying was a close second to these transgressions.

A fter World War I, Rabbi Boruch Ber Lebovitz wished to return to Poland from Russia. He was stopped at the border and asked whether he was a Polish citizen. Admitting that he was not would jeopardize his entire future. Rabbi Boruch Ber could not get himself to lie and said, "I am *not a citizen of Poland, but I have many students in Poland." The border guards were struck by his refusal to lie, and respectfully allowed him to enter Poland.*

～～

Just how cautious our Torah giants were to avoid even the remotest trace of falsehood can be seen in an episode in the life of Rabbi Yechezkel Levenstein, who was asked to deliver a eulogy at the funeral of the dean of the Slabodka Yeshivah. To everyone's surprise, Rabbi Levenstein refused, and later explained his reluctance. Shortly before this, he had suffered a tragic loss with the death of a beloved grandchild, and would cry when reminded of this. "During the eulogy," he said, "I might have been moved to tears because of my own loss. However, the audience would think that I was crying because of the death of this Torah scholar, and this would not be true. I could not put myself in a position where I would be giving people a false impression."

Just how loathsome lying is from a Torah's perspective can be seen from a comment by Rabbi Yeshaya Karelitz (the Chazon Ish), who once heard a person exclaim "That is *sheker* (a lie)." The Chazon Ish took him aside and said softly to him, "The very word *sheker* is an abomination and should not be used. What you may say is, 'That is untrue.'"

Although the Scriptural prohibition of lying appears to be only for *verbalizing* a falsehood, King David extends this to require truth *in thought*. He cites among the virtues that will merit being in the Divine presence: "one who speaks truth in his heart "(*Psalms* 15:2). We need not go back to Talmudic times for an example of this.

R eb Shraga Feivel Frank, the father-in-law of
Rabbi Issar Zalman Meltzer, dealt in leather.
A customer wished to purchase a large quantity of leather, and because of the size of the purchase, asked for a discount. Reb Shraga Feivel replied that he does not give volume discounts, and the customer was free to go elsewhere to get a better deal. He gave the man a list of other dealers in leather.

After making the rounds of the other dealers, the man realized that Reb Shraga Feivel's price was in fact the lowest, and he returned to buy the leather from him at the quoted price. To his surprise, Reb Shraga Feivel said he would give him the discount he had requested.

"I don't understand you," the customer said. "When I initially asked for a discount, you refused even though you expected that I would buy elsewhere. But now that I am coming back to buy at your price, you offer me a discount! This doesn't make sense."

Rabbi Shraga Feivel explained, "After you left I realized that even with a discount, I would have made a decent profit on the volume you wanted, and that it was foolish of me to be so rigid on the price. Essentially, I had agreed in my heart to accept a lower price. In the morning davening we say that a person should speak the truth in his heart. How could I pray these words tomorrow morning if I did not do what I had agreed to in my heart?"

This, then, is spiritual man: A person who is striving for spiritual perfection, and since this is his *true* being, that which G–d intended him to be by creating him to be a *mentsch*, he cannot tolerate anything that is false, neither in his speech nor in his thought.

18
Resentment Without Cause

e have noted that there are some negative traits, such as lying, that are unique to the human being, and that spirituality consists of suppressing these traits. This is also true of another trait by which humans may unfortunately be plagued, which is to resent someone without cause. The consequences of this trait can be most tragic. Indeed, the Talmud states that the Second Temple was destroyed because there was *sinas chinam,* causeless resentment among the Jews.

But how can something like *sinas chinam* exist? Why in the world would a person feel hostile toward someone who has never offended or harmed him? After all, we are more or less rational creatures, and resenting someone without cause is totally senseless.

We may be helped to understand this phenomenon by virtue of knowing something about the workings of the human psyche. Our conscious mind is indeed guided by laws of logic, but there is another portion of our mind which does not follow the laws of logic at all, and this is our *unconscious*. When we are asleep, our conscious mind is not functioning, and it is the unconscious which produces our dreams. We all know how totally absurd our dreams may be, and this is because the unconscious mind takes fragments of data and throws them together every which way, resulting in scenes that can be internally contradictory and illogical.

Nevertheless, the unconscious does have some rules of its own, and we are aware of a few of these. One rule of the unconscious is that "the part equals the whole." In other words, whereas the conscious mind adheres to the principle that "quantities that are equal to the same quantity are equal to each other" (if a= b and b=c, then a=c), the unconscious holds that if *part* of "a" equals *part* of "b," then a=b. This is an absurdity, because it can lead to the conclusion that if my house is made of brick and Buckingham Palace is made of brick, then my house is Buckingham Palace. To the conscious mind this is ridiculous, but the unconscious mind operates by rather ridiculous laws.

It is also important to realize that the unconscious mind can have a powerful impact on the emotions, which explains why we are capable of having feelings that do not appear to be logically warranted.

We have probably all had the experience of meeting someone for the very first time and feeling an immediate antipathy toward him, although there cannot be the slightest justification for this feeling. It is possible that something about this person, perhaps a facial feature, a mannerism, a tone of voice, or even a piece of clothing he is wearing, elicits a memory of someone we disliked who also had that particular feature. For the unconscious this is enough to establish an identity, and the unconscious equates the two, so that this person whom we just met is perceived by the unconscious as the person we had once disliked, and this generates a hostile feeling toward him. This is how *sinas chinam* may develop.

However, the human mind takes this one step further. The conscious mind may be perplexed by this negative feeling, but instead of rejecting it as absurd and erroneous, may try to justify it by *rationalization*. The person then begins to give himself quasi-logical reasons why this person should be disliked, and, of course, we are prone to believe our rationalizations. Before too long, we may build up a case against this person which is totally unfounded in reality.

Sinas chinam provides an unusual opportunity for the *yetzer hara*, which is always on the lookout for ways in which it can cause divisiveness among Jews. The *yetzer hara* may utilize the mechanism of rationalization to fabricate more and more reasons to justify the hostile feelings.

We must therefore be on the alert not to fall into the trap of *sinas chinam*. Even when someone has in fact offended us, we should have the *middos* to overcome resentment, and certainly so when the resentment is totally groundless.

Even if the human being were a *Homo sapiens* in the most restrictive definition of intellect, *sinas chinam* is a trait which we must overcome. It is the highest degree of folly to allow ourselves to despise someone without valid reason. A spiritual person goes even beyond the demands of pure intellect, hence he should be free of any and all resentments.

Justice

The rule of the jungle is "might is right." Whether due to limited food and water or other factors, the weakest among the wild perish. There is no system to protect the weak. Human beings must be governed by principles of justice, hence one must be just to be spiritual.

Justice is a pillar of Judaism, as is stated in *Ethics of the Fathers* (1:18). It is true that other peoples also have a system of laws, but the concept of justice as taught by Torah is substantially different, because justice in Judaism is based on unalterable principles of Divine origin that are not subject to manipulation by society to meet its own needs. History has examples of systems of law that were anything but humane, such as the legendary corrupt laws of Sodom, or, in our own time, the laws adopted in Nazi Germany, which not only deprived Jews of social rights, but declared their very right to live null and void, leading to the atrocities of the Holocaust which were far more decadent than the behavior of brute beasts.

Torah authorities must execute justice within the limits provided by the Torah, but may not abrogate Torah law, regardless of what may be thought to be advantageous to society. No court and no legislature can legalize anything forbidden by the Torah.

Although being governed by law is a uniquely human trait, it cannot be considered a spiritual trait when it is centripetal, and it is of little account whether the "self" toward which a behavior is directed is the individual or society. Whatever is primarily centripetal in nature is lacking in spirituality.

We do not have to go back to Biblical history or even to several decades ago to see distortions of justice. This very day legislatures and courts across the country are legalizing behaviors which were abhorrent just a short while back, and this system of "justice," which would be impossible under Torah law, can hardly be said to contribute to spirituality.

The Torah repeatedly stresses the need to look after the needs of the poor, the weak, and the underprivileged. Regardless of what the majority of people may prefer, Torah law cannot condone euthanasia, deviant behavior, or abortion unless the latter is to save the life of the mother.

Rabbi Moshe Feinstein points out an important difference between punishment in secular law and punishment in Torah. The law punishes a criminal primarily to deter him and others from harming society with their criminal behavior. This is why rehabilitation efforts in prison have been repeatedly fraught with failure. The purpose of imprisonment never was to help the person become a better person, but to protect society. Hence, the person who cares little about the rights of others when he enters prison is apt to feel the same way when he is released, and will return to his previous ways. In Torah, however, the primary purpose of punishment is to help the person realize that his behavior was wrong so that he *can become a better person.*

The character of Torah-based justice may be seen by citing just one example of Torah law. Suppose a poor person were to sue a very wealthy person, and when the two appear before the *beis din* (rabbinic tribunal), the poor person is dressed in very simple clothes, whereas the wealthy man is wearing a custom-made suit, a monogrammed shirt, alligator leather shoes, and is sporting a diamond ring. He is instructed, "Either you buy the poor person clothes equal to those you are wearing, or you dress in simple clothes like him." If one of the litigants appears more impressive than the other, this may cause the judges to lean toward him in their judgment.

On the other hand, the law may not be circumvented out of consideration for the poor, and if the verdict should favor the wealthy person, the judge may not reason, "What difference would a paltry few hundred dollars make to this multi-millionaire? For this poor person, it may make the difference between having something to eat or starving." The law must be applied justly. It is related that when such a case came before King David, he would rule justly, and then see to it that the needs of the poor person were cared for, but not at the cost of ruling contrary to law. There are numerous accounts of similar actions by rabbinic courts throughout Jewish history.

The pivotal role of justice as a criterion for humanity is stated in the Midrash, which relates that prior to creation of man, G–d sought counsel of the heavenly angels. Some discouraged G–d from creating man, because man would be prone to lie and to quarrel, whereas others favored creation of man because he would be just (*Bereishis Rabbah* 8:5). It is thus evident that justice is considered an essential component of humanity, hence also of spirituality.

The Torah attitude toward justice is illustrated in a story I heard from my father.

In a town in Eastern Europe there were two prominent Torah scholars. One was Rabbi Chajkel, the religious leader of the community, and the other, Rabbi Azriel, served as the dayan (magistrate). The two were bosom friends, and spent many hours together in Torah study.

One time the two were learning together when a woman came in and asked Rabbi Chajkel to please hold 500 rubles for her in safekeeping, since she was leaving town for several days and there was no other place in town where she felt her money would be safe.

When the woman returned for her money, Rabbi Chajkel was unable to locate it. He searched all the drawers and cabinets in the house, and went through the pockets of every article of clothing he owned, but to no avail. The money was gone. He asked Rabbi Azriel whether he had seen where he had put the money, but Rabbi Azriel said he had been engrossed in his study and had not paid any attention.

It occurred to Rabbi Chajkel that several weeks earlier Rabbi Azriel had mentioned that he was most distressed because he had a daughter of marriageable age, but he was encountering difficulty in finding an appropriate husband for her because he could not provide a dowry. Rabbi Chajkel knew that Rabbi Azriel was honest to a fault, but he was obsessed by the thought that Rabbi Azriel might have been so overwhelmed by his compassion for his child that he could not resist taking the money.

With a heavy heart, Rabbi Chajkel said to his friend, "My beloved friend, I know that this is absurd, yet you and I were the only two people in the room. I know that you are beyond suspicion, but the woman is demanding her money, and since you were the only person who could have had access to it, the halachah requires that you take an oath that you did not take the money."

Rabbi Azriel turned pale. "Rabbi Chajkel," he said, "please let me think about this a bit." That evening Rabbi Azriel came to Rabbi Chajkel's home and said, "Here is 275 rubles. That is all I have."

Rabbi Chajkel, knowing that Rabbi Azriel did not possess that sum, had his suspicions reinforced. Where would Rabbi Azriel have amassed such a sum otherwise? With a firm tone he said, "I'm sorry, Rabbi Azriel. The amount is 500."

"Give me one more day," Rabbi Azriel pleaded. The following day Rabbi Azriel brought an additional 125 rubles. Rabbi Chajkel became stern. "I must have the entire 500, Rabbi Azriel," he said.

"I do not have a single kopeck more," Rabbi Azriel said. "Please ask the woman to accept a promissory note." The woman agreed to do so.

Rabbi Chajkel did not speak to his formerly bosom friend again, and if he met Rabbi Azriel in the street he would turn away. He was deeply grieved that his trusted friend had been unable to withstand temptation and had resorted to theft.

Eventually Passover approached, and in cleaning his study for the holiday, Rabbi Chajkel moved the she'visi (a plaque reminding one that G–d is present everywhere), and out fell the bundle of money! This is where he had placed it that day, but it had not occurred to him to look for it there. Realizing how cruel he had been to Rabbi Azriel, he emitted a loud shriek and fainted.

When he was revived, Rabbi Chajkel wept bitterly, tore at his beard, and beat his head against the wall. What had he done? He had accused the saintly Rabbi Azriel of being a thief! He could not be consoled. He ran to the synagogue where the townsfolk had gathered for Minchah (afternoon prayer), stepped to the pulpit, and while crying profusely shouted, "Dear people! I am no longer your Rabbi. I do not deserve to be even your janitor. I am a scoundrel! I have aggrieved a tzaddik! I do not deserve to walk on the face of the earth!" He then ran to the Ark, threw open its doors, and shouted, "Only You, G–d, can forgive me."

Just then Rabbi Azriel entered the synagogue. Rabbi Chajkel ran to him, fell to the ground and took hold of his feet. "Forgive me, holy friend. Please find it in your heart to forgive me! Given the circumstances, I was bound by halachah to require you to swear. But I was so wrong. I should have known better!"

Rabbi Azriel helped his friend to his feet and warmly embraced him. "Rabbi Chajkel," he said, "there was never any need for forgiveness. You merely did what halachah required you to do. You had no other recourse.

"I have never, in all my life, taken an oath," Rabbi Azriel said. "When you told me that halachah required me to swear, I shuddered. I therefore took the 250 rubles I had borrowed for my daughter's wedding, and sold whatever trinkets my wife had for another 25 rubles.

"When you told me that was not enough, I sold my library for 125 rubles. I am so grateful to you, Rabbi Chajkel, that you prevailed upon the woman to accept my promissory note for the balance. I am so grateful, because I do not know what I would have done had she not done so. To swear, even when you know you are swearing the truth, is awesome. You spared me the anguish of taking an oath, and for that I shall forever be grateful."

Yes, we had spiritual people. Rabbi Azriel was a magistrate, and when the Talmud states that G–d is present in the *beis din*, we can readily understand why. G–d must have profound pleasure when He observes judges like Rabbi Azriel implementing the law of the Torah.

Instinct vs. Intellect

Rambam poses a question: According to the account in the Torah, the forbidden fruit in *Gan Eden* would enable a person to distinguish between good and evil. Indeed, after Adam and Eve ate of the fruit, "their eyes opened" (*Genesis* 3:7); i.e., they were now able to distinguish between good and evil. How is it possible, asks Rambam, that a sin should result in acquiring the ability to distinguish between good and evil?

Rambam answers that prior to the sin, Adam and Eve had no need to distinguish between good and evil, because they avoided evil by instinct. Just as animals instinctively avoid vegetation that is poisonous, so were Adam and Eve endowed with the instinct to avoid evil. When they sinned, they lost this intuitive protection against evil, and would now have to distinguish between good and evil by means of intellect. Clearly, instinct is much more efficient than intellect, because instinct of that caliber (Divinely ordained) is not subject to error, whereas intellectual judgment is fraught with the possibility of error. The consequence of the sin was thus a loss rather than a gain.

[The obvious question is then, how did the sin come about if Adam and Eve had an instinctive barrier against anything that was forbidden? A possible answer is that because Adam and Eve were aware of their instinct, when they heard the Divine statement that the fruit of the Tree of Wisdom should not be eaten, they assumed that since it was forbidden it was *inedible*, and they hardly needed to take precautions to avoid anything that would naturally repel them. Satan, however, in the form of the serpent, was able to delude them so they would see the fruit as "good for eating" (*Genesis* 3:6), and Adam and Eve assumed that if they had a desire for the fruit, this must not be the tree which G–d had forbidden, because otherwise they would not have had a desire for it. Their sin was that they were not on guard against Satan's seductive powers to delude people and make the inedible appear tasty.]

It is possible, however, to acquire a quasi-instinct. For example, there are cultures which consider locusts to be a delicacy, which is nothing less than nauseating to Western civilization because we consider them repulsive. Additionally, an infant does not know that bugs are loathsome, and will not hesitate to pick up a bug and place it in his mouth. When his mother sees him do this, her reaction of disgust is so violent that it leaves an indelible impression on the child, and for the rest of his life he feels that bugs are revolting. He no longer has to resist his inborn temptation to eat bugs, because they have essentially become "instinctively" abhorrent.

It is possible to develop a quasi-instinct against things that are forbidden. For example, an observant Jew does not have to muster up resistance against eating pork, because just the thought of it is abhorrent. Should he pass by a *tereifah* food vendor when he is hungry, he will not have to exert any effort to resist temptation, because he is not in the least tempted to eat *tereifah*.

In *Michtav MeEliyahu,* Rabbi Dessler states that a person should make more and more forbidden things repulsive, so that he does even have to actively resist them. Rabbi Dessler states that the struggle with the *yetzer hara* is very much like a battle between two hostile forces. They may begin fighting at a particular battlefront, but as one of them triumphs and conquers enemy territory, the front is pushed forward to a new site where the battle now takes place, and the conquered area is secure, with no struggle occurring there. As one force continues to win, the battlefront is constantly advanced, with more and more conquered territory becoming secure.

This, says Rabbi Dessler, is how the battle against the *yetzer hara* should advance. A person who observes

Shabbos would not even remotely consider turning on a light or driving the car on Shabbos. This area of Shabbos observance is secure. However, it is also forbidden to talk about business on Shabbos, and it is not beyond possibility that he may discuss a business deal on Shabbos with a friend (sometimes even in *shul*). When it is brought to his attention in a *halachah shiur* that this is wrong, he may resolve not to do so again, and the next time the opportunity arises to talk about business on Shabbos, he may make a conscious effort to restrain himself. At this point, talking about business on Shabbos is not beyond possibility the way turning on a light is. According to Rabbi Dessler, a person should learn more about the great sanctity of Shabbos, and develop so great a reverence for it that he no longer needs to exert restraint to avoid talking about business on Shabbos. It just cannot happen.

Rabbi Dessler states that this is the kind of progression that should occur in the observance of Torah. Since we do have *bechirah* (free choice), we are capable of putting more and more things beyond us, so that they no longer will require active *bechirah* any more than does the avoidance of pork. As in a war, we should constantly advance the front against the foe, in this case the *yetzer hara,* so that more and more territory will be "secure."

If we follow this to its logical conclusion, it is theoretically possible to achieve a state of an essentially instinctive avoidance of sin, similar to that of Adam and Eve before the sin. While this may be beyond reach, it should nevertheless be the goal. As humans, we may never achieve perfection, but we should aim for it nevertheless.

Rabbi Dessler's teaching can be applied to every component of spirituality. Ironically, in this case man should aspire to be *like* animals; i.e., to instinctively avoid anything that is toxic to spirituality. What would then distinguish man from animals is that the latter were created with their instinct, while man must achieve this instinct by exercising his intellect. As we said earlier, G–d created animals in a state of completion, but man must work to develop his perfection, which is the ultimate of spirituality.

The Growth Pattern of Spirituality

piritual growth is somewhat similar to physical growth, in that there are periods of rapid growth spurts and periods of apparent stagnation. As in physical growth, the latter are actually periods of latency, where the groundwork is being laid for another rapid growth phase.

Spiritual growth differs from physical growth in two ways: (1) It never comes to completion; and (2) there are periods when one feels he has regressed rather than progressed. The latter can be very frustrating and disappointing unless it is correctly understood. We have all had times when we feel we have prayed well with a great deal of *kavanah* (concentration) or studied a page of the Talmud with a profound sensation of being in contact with the Divine wisdom, but when we try to duplicate these feelings the next day, we find that they are not retrievable.

One of the Baal Shem Tov's students complained that he was feeling frustrated. "I try to get close to G–d," he said, "but just when I feel I am about to make contact, I suddenly find myself cast away far from Him."

The Baal Shem Tov smiled and said, "Of course, my child, that is just how it should be.

"Imagine the scene of a father who wishes to teach his infant child how to walk. He waits until the child can stand upright, but the child hesitates to take the first step for fear of falling. Until then, he was firmly balanced on all fours, but walking on two feet seems very risky.

"The father places himself near the child, and extends his arms very close to him, beckoning him to come. The child wishes to reach the father, and seeing the father's hands close enough to catch him if he were to totter, he has the courage to take the first step.

"What does the father do? He moves back a bit, still close enough so that the child will feel unafraid. Having successfully taken the first step and seeing the father close enough, the child ventures the second step. This time the father moves farther back, and continues moving ever farther away as the child takes more steps.

"If we were to read the infant's mind, we would no doubt find him thinking, 'What is going on here? The harder I try to reach my father, the farther away from me he is.'

"What is going on is that the child and the father have divergent goals. The child's goal is to reach the father. The father's goal is to teach the child how to ambulate independently. Certainly the father wishes to embrace his beloved child, but the moment he does so, the lesson is over and the progress ceases.

"So it is with you, who wish to reach G–d. However, G–d's wish is that you grow spiritually, and such growth can occur only as long as you are striving for Him. The moment you reach Him, your growth stops.

"In this world we grow by striving, and we can therefore never feel we have reached G–d. In the World to Come, where there is no further growth, G–d will embrace us and we will feel we have indeed reached Him."

This principle is extremely important to bear in mind, because without it, the periods of frustration may result in depression. We must remember that in order for us to merit the Divine reward, we must endure a struggle, and that the *yetzer hara* (evil instinct) was placed within us by G–d as the force which we must overcome. The *yetzer hara* is extremely cunning, and may utilize the moments of frustration to throw us into a state of despair and resignation. We may think, "What is the use of trying? Whenever I achieve a feeling of spirituality, it quickly disappears. All this effort is futile." This is the machination of the *yetzer hara,* and we must be aware of it. The parable of the Baal Shem Tov should enable us to identify the times we feel distant from G–d as growth periods, whereby G–d wishes us to strive ever more vigorously to reach Him.

It is important to be aware that the *yetzer hara,* while trying to obstruct our spiritual progress, and while using every conceivable tactic to achieve this, actually wishes that we do not obey him. Rabbi Shneur Zalman quotes a parable from the *Zohar* to demonstrate this point:

A *king wished to test the moral fiber of his son, and he therefore hired a woman to try and lead the prince astray. The woman knew that she must obey the king and that she must do her utmost, using every strategy available to trap the prince. However, she secretly hoped that the prince would withstand the trial and not succumb.*

So it is with the *yetzer hara,* which is an agent created by G–d to seduce us to sin. The *yetzer hara* does his job faithfully, but really wishes that we do not listen to him.

An additional aid to help us resist the *yetzer hara* is provided by yet another parable of the Baal Shem Tov:

A *king who wished to test the loyalty of his subjects engaged a very cunning person to go among the people and incite them to rebellion, presenting them with evidence of how the king treats them unjustly, and how much better off they would be if they threw off the yoke of being his subjects.*

Some fools were taken in by this person's clever arguments. The wise, however, said, "How could it possibly be that so powerful a king would permit someone to circulate and incite against him. That is absurd! Clearly this is nothing but a ruse, a trial whereby the king wishes to test our loyalty to him, and therefore allows this to happen."

Wise people recognize the *yetzer hara* as being an agent of G–d, put there to test us. It is the height of folly to think that there is any substance to the *yetzer hara's* inciting us to disobey G–d.

Combining these parables, the increasing distance that the father assumes relative to the child's progress in walking represents the ever increasing force of the *yetzer hara* as we grow spiritually. The Talmud states this very clearly: "The greater the person, the stronger is his *yetzer hara*" (*Succah* 52a). A person with little spirituality has a relatively weaker *yetzer hara* than someone of greater spirituality. As we have noted with the tests of the patriarch Abraham our struggles may increase rather than decrease in severity as we grow in spirituality. If we recognize this pattern, we will be in a much better position to triumph.

There is yet another important alert. To be stagnant is one thing, and even the appearance of regression can be tolerated. However, it is also possible for a person to descend into the depths of degeneracy, from which he sees no hope of ever emerging. One must keep in mind that there is no such thing as despair in Judaism. The Talmud relates the episode of Elazar ben Doradia whose entire life was one of profligacy, and who was suddenly shocked into the awareness of his decadence. Even this far-advanced case was not hopeless, and in one single moment of sincere *teshuvah*, he gained entry to Paradise (*Avodah Zarah* 17a).

Let me borrow from my experience in treating alcoholics. These people, who have been trapped in a vicious cycle of escaping misery or seeking a "high" via alcohol, may not emerge from their self-destructive addiction until they reach a "rock-bottom," some kind of experience which breaks through their denial and opens their eyes to their sorry state. As dreadful as the "rock-bottom" experience may be, it must be viewed as being the turning point in their lives from which they can begin their recovery. This may also be true of the path to spirituality, upon which some people may not embark until they have descended into the depths of hedonism or even depravity.

For those who see no way of attaining spirituality, I wish to suggest a metaphor which I again have borrowed from a recovering alcoholic. This man was 35 years away from his last drink when he told this story.

"I had lost everything due to my drinking, and I had nowhere to go but up, but I didn't have the slightest idea what to do. Two guys who had stopped drinking tried to convince me to follow the program of Alcoholics Anonymous and told me that this would help me regain my life. I couldn't imagine what they were talking about.

"I felt like I was standing at the bank of a river, wanting to get across to the other side, when two guys came along and said, 'If you want to get across, start rowing.' I looked at them in bewilderment and said, 'But there is no boat!' They said, 'Just start rowing. The boat will appear.' I thought they were out of their minds, but I was so desperate that I did what they said, and followed the recommended program. As a result of that, I am now 35 years sober, and happier than I have ever been."

RaMChaL in *Mesillas Yesharim* (*Path of the Just*) uses the metaphor of a person who is in a maze and is trying to get to the goal, but has no way of knowing which is the correct path. On a high platform there is a person who can see the entire maze, and who shouts directions. "Don't try that path," he shouts, "it leads to nowhere! Follow the path that I will show you." How foolish one would be not to listen.

There are excellent guides in Torah literature on spirituality. The works of *mussar* and *chassidus* tell us which paths to avoid and which to pursue to reach the desired goal. We would be wise to follow their direction.

Humility

I
s it possible for an animal to be humble? Most probably not. We may therefore add *humility* to the list of features that are uniquely human.

The importance of humility can be gathered from the fact that the only praise the Torah mentions with regard to Moses is: "He was the most humble of all people" (*Numbers* 12:3). Reflect on this for a moment. Moses, the greatest of all prophets, who had reached the ultimate of spiritual heights, and of whom the Midrash says, "He was part human, part angel" (*Shocher Tov* 90:5), without doubt excelled in many admirable traits. Yet, all the Torah tells us about his character is that he was humble.

"Humility encompasses all other desirable traits, and is the key to all these traits" (*Tomer Devorah* 2). "If a person is humble, he divests himself of all negative traits, because the latter all stem from vanity" (*Shulchan HaTahor* 84:2). In his last will, Rambam says, "Humility is the ladder to reach G–d."

In most of my writings I refer to the importance of self-esteem in developing a healthy personality. Invariably some people ask, "But is not self-esteem contrary to humility?" The answer is a most emphatic "no." Not only is self-esteem compatible with humility, but indeed, humility can be achieved only by someone who has self-esteem.

Self-esteem means that a person has a sense of worthiness and is aware of his capabilities. Since every person has a *neshamah,* which, as we have seen, is part of G–d himself, then every person has an inherent worthiness. In addition, every person has strengths which can be put to constructive use. To know the truth about oneself is not vanity, and humility does not mean denying one's capabilities.

The Torah testifies to Moses' profound humility. Did Moses not know that he was the only human who spoke directly with G–d? Did he not recognize that he was chosen as the leader of Israel, and that he performed unparalleled miracles? Of course Moses was aware of his enormous capacities, but these did not go to his head. From Moses to the Chafetz Chaim, our great Torah personalities clearly knew their competence in Torah, else they would not have written authoritative works on *halachah.*

The noted ethicist, Rabbi Yehudah Leib Chasman, said: "It is obvious that humility does not mean denying one's capabilities. That would be folly rather than humility" (*Ohr Yahel 3; Shemini*). Rabbi Yeruchem Levovitz says, "A person who does not recognize his defects is at a disadvantage, because he does not know what he must correct. But someone who is not aware of his capabilities is far worse off, because he does not even know what tools he has to work with" (*Tikkun HaMiddos,* On Humility, page 164). Self-effacement does not mean denial of the truth about oneself.

Some people, for whatever reason, have a poor self-image and very low self-esteem. They think of themselves as inferior and unworthy, and these feelings can be so distressing that they may have recourse to various mechanisms in an attempt to escape this pain. I dealt with this subject at length in *Life's Too Short* (*St. Martins Press*).

One of the methods a person with low self-esteem may employ to escape the torment of feeling inferior is to imagine he is better than everyone else. He is likely to be a braggart, boasting of his accomplishments to everyone, or pursuing honor and acclaim. He is easily offended, and he is the person whom you place at the head of the list of your invitees, not because you like him so much, but because if you were to accidentally omit him, you would never hear the end of it. He is the person who is slighted if not accorded what he considers to be the proper honor in the *shul,* or if not seated near the head table at a banquet. This is a description of a vain person. Thus, paradoxically, a vain person is not one who really thinks he is great, but, to the contrary, one who feels so inferior that he seeks validation and reassurance from others, and develops a delusion of grandiosity. The vain person is unhappy, because his desire to be recognized and appreciated is a bottomless pit, and he is never satisfied.

It is only the person with a healthy self-esteem, who feels worthy as a child of G–d and who is aware of his G–d-given strengths and talents, that can be humble and self-effacing because he does not need the desperate defense of vanity. Hence, self-esteem is not only compatible with humility, but is actually a necessary prerequisite for it.

Torah considers vanity so despicable a trait that G–d is quoted as saying, "One of haughty eyes and expansive heart, him I cannot bear" (*Psalms* 101:5). Although Torah ethics recommends avoiding all extremes, and the Rambam advocates "The Golden Path" or the mean of virtue as the ideal measure for all character traits, a notable exception to this is humility, about which it is said: "Be very, very humble" (*Ethics of the Fathers* 4:4), so that one should not have even the slightest trace of vanity.

All this notwithstanding, there are situations when one must set humility aside and assert oneself rather than defer, and these are in regard to observing the will of G–d. Here one must hold fast to one's opinion and champion the cause rather than yield to the opinion of others.

The Talmud states that although both King Saul and King David sinned, David was forgiven, whereas Saul was not. The incident with Saul involved his failure to destroy all the booty of the vanquished Amalekites as the prophet Samuel had instructed him. When rebuked by Samuel, Saul said that he yielded to the populace, who wished to retain the livestock to be used for sacrificial offerings to G–d. Samuel's admonition serves as a teaching for all times: "If you are humble in your eyes (you must remember that) you are the head of the children of Israel" (*I Samuel* 15:17). In other words, this was a time when you should have exercised your authority as king, rather than your profound humility which caused you to yield to the wishes of the people. Misguided humility can be destructive, and there are times when even lay people must assume a position of leadership and authority if the Divine will is being challenged.

Earlier we noted that spirituality requires a person to reflect on the purpose of his existence, and that Judaism is based on the belief that G–d created the universe for a purpose known only to Him. By giving us the Torah, G–d made His will known to us, and it is our purpose to follow His commandments.

It is a tenet of faith that G–d is in every way infinite, and this is expressed in the kabbalistic term for G–d: *Ein Sof* (Without End). The human mind is unable to fully grasp the terms "eternity" and "infinity," since there is nothing in our experience that is without beginning or end. The best we can do with infinity is to try to imagine a vast expanse, and even this is difficult. Astronomers tell us that there are countless galaxies, some of which are millions of light years distant. If we realize that light travels at 186,000 miles per second, and that a "light day" is a distance of 16,070,400,000 miles, we can hardly imagine the distance of a light year, which is 365 times that, and the idea of something being a million light years distant is a quantity so great that it is actually meaningless. Yet, even these astronomical distances fade into nothingness in relation to infinity. In terms of the expanse of the universe known to science, the entire solar system is no more than a single drop of water in the Pacific Ocean, and our planet Earth a mere tiny fraction of that. If a person thinks of the concept of infinity, one's own being shrinks into virtual nothingness.

Yet, it is our faith that the *Ein Sof* chose this infinitesimal planet upon which to place man, and that man has a mission to fulfill the Divine will here on earth. Our Torah scholars tell us that although we cannot grasp it, fulfilling this mission on tiny earth actually sustains the entire universe. The Talmud states that humble man is required to think, "The universe was created for me" (*Sanhedrin* 37a); i.e., to give me the ability to carry out the Divine will. G–d has bestowed an immeasurable greatness on this bit of nothingness, and by faith, both concepts are compatible.

Early idolatry was prompted by the concept that infinite G–d would not be interested in such infinitesimally insignificant creatures as humans, hence he must have assigned the care of lesser worlds to underlings who must be appeased by worship. Judaism teaches that G–d is interested in everything a person does, and that every human is the object of Divine providence. To G–d, a super galaxy and a tiny molecule are of equal importance, because in relationship to infinity, larger and smaller quantities are either both significant or both insignificant. Two divided by zero and one billion divided by zero are both equal. The Talmud states that we repeatedly find references in the Scriptures to prove the fact that an infinitely great G–d attends to the needs of the least of His creatures (*Megillah* 31a).

A person should be extremely humble, yet feel a great responsibility for fulfilling his mission on earth, which is to strive for spiritual perfection. We know full well that perfection is not attainable, yet we must strive for it, as stated: "It is not incumbent upon you to complete the task (reaching perfection), yet you are not free to shirk it" (*Ethics of the Fathers* 2:16). Since one is to strive for a goal that is constantly receding, one is humbled by the relatively small amount that one has accomplished. However, this is not at all like the sense of despair that accompanies futility, but rather a stimulus to ambition, to reach ever further and higher. Our great Torah personalities were humbled by the awareness of how small a piece of infinity they had attained, yet they always strove for more.

The chassidic master, Rabbi Bunim of Peshis'cha, took himself to task for what he felt were his character defects. He said, "When I appear before the heavenly tribunal they will ask me, 'Bunim, did you study Torah adequately?' And I will say, 'No, I did not have sufficient intellect to grasp Torah properly.' They will ask, 'Bunim, did you do mitzvos properly?' And I will say 'No, I was preoccupied with earning a living,

and did not have sufficient time for proper per-
formance of mitzvos.' They will say, 'Bunim, did
you give adequate tzedakah?' And I will say,
'No, I did not have enough money to give much
tzedakah.' Then will come the awesome ques-
tion, 'Bunim, if you were lax in the study of
Torah and performance of mitzvos and did not
give proper tzedakah, on what basis were you
vain?' Alas, to this question I will have no an-
swer." Rabbi Bunim also said, "I constantly
thank G–d that vanity is not a mitzvah, because
if it were, what is there about myself that would
allow me to be vain?"

We have already eluded to *sheker* (falsehood) as being reprehensible, and inasmuch as there is no basis in
reality for a person to be vain, all vanity is false, and
both are abominable traits. Their toxicity to spirituality
may be compared to a single microscopic bacteria,
which may reproduce itself to the point that it can kill a
person. Similarly, even a touch of vanity may so affect a
person that it may destroy every vestige of spirituality.

Again we turn to the lives of our *tzaddikim,* who ac-
tualized in their daily lives the principles of spirituality
we have described.

R*abbi Akiva Eiger, who was recognized by*
Torah scholars as one of the greatest
Talmudists of all time, once came to Warsaw,
and the learned notables of the city came out to
greet him to show their respect for this out-
standing person. Rabbi Akiva wept profusely,

and when asked for the cause of his crying, he said, "How far down have we fallen! How impoverished our generation must be, that someone like myself is regarded as a scholar. If our generation had true scholars, they would realize how little I know."

⁓⁓

Rabbi Menachem Kaplan of Horodna served as the caretaker of a small synagogue, which provided him with a wage that was beneath the poverty level. His wife, who was aware of his mastery of Torah, pleaded with him to accept a position as a Rabbi of a larger community, for which he was more than qualified. Rabbi Menachem said, "But think what will happen when people discover how deficient I am in Torah knowledge. Can you imagine the embarrassment we will both suffer?" Rabbi Menachem's wife realized that given his humility, she was pleading a lost cause. Only later was his enormous erudition revealed to the world.

⁓⁓

The greatness of the Chafetz Chaim was equaled only by his profound humility. When he was accorded great respect, he lamented, "What wrong have I done that I have been punished with being considered a Torah scholar? People will expect of me the kind of behavior that *is proper for a learned person, and I cannot live up to that!" These words from a tzaddik whose Torah knowledge and saintliness are legendary.*

⁀⁀

Rabbi Yisrael Hagar of Viznitz was traveling in a coach, and the driver boasted about his skill managing the horses. "I learned this trade from my father, who was an excellent coachman," he said. The Rabbi sighed. "You have followed in your father's footsteps and perhaps even surpassed him. What can I say? My father was a scholar and a tzaddik, but I have amounted to nothing."

It is really little wonder that our prominent Torah scholars were paragons of humility. What we are pathetically unaware of are the countless numbers of great Torah scholars who succeeded in concealing their greatness, and because they were not catapulted into positions of leadership, many have remained unsung heroes. With some of these, their secret was discovered after their demise, and they were spared the distress of fame.

In our own generation there was a milkman in Jerusalem who would push his milk cart along the narrow streets of the Holy City, while reciting by heart the many pages of Talmud he had memorized. It is related that Rabbi Aaron Kotler once met him and they engaged in a complex

Talmudic dialogue for hours. Rabbi Kotler could not believe that this outstanding scholar was only a milkman.

≈≈

In the Meah Shearim section of Jerusalem lived Reb Dov, as he was known to all. His mornings were spent providing for the needs of the poor, and particularly of those individuals in the community who were neglected because of their compromised mentality and irrational behavior. Reb Dov made sure that the mentally ill had what to eat and where to sleep.

After his prayers he would study Torah, and was often interrupted by people who sought his counsel. More than once he ate breakfast while others were eating supper, because his time was taken up by the services he provided to others, which took priority over his own needs.

After his death, many manuscripts of his were found, volumes of commentary on various aspects of Torah. The community had indeed appreciated him as a wise and benevolent person, but no one dreamed of his greatness in Torah knowledge until he was beyond being a "victim" of acclaim and praise.

No one can claim that such levels of spirituality are no longer attainable in modern times. These people lived quite recently. The striving for spiritual perfection is not in any way affected by the calendar.

Sanctity of Speech

e have already noted that spirituality means elevating ourselves above the animal level, and certainly to avoid descending below that level. But that is precisely what happens too often when we abuse the gift of speech.

Animals, too, have a way of communicating, and the unintelligible sounds they make undoubtedly can be understood by other animals. The Torah states that when G–d breathed a spirit of life into man, he became a "living soul" (*Genesis* 2:8), which Onkeles translates as "a spirit that can speak." Granted that man probably has a much broader vocabulary than animals, but since animals also have a way of verbal communication, why is this trait so unique to man that Onkeles considers it as *the* identifying feature of man?

The answer is that it is not the simple power of speech that defines man, but rather his capability of using that power appropriately, and in particular, his capability of resisting the temptation to abuse that power.

When a person speaks vulgar language, he is abusing this special gift of G–d, and this is an affront to G–d. As Onkeles indicates, it was the spirit which G–d "breathed" into Adam that gave him his uniqueness as man. As we have previously noted, the *Zohar* points out that when someone breathes out, he exhales something from within himself, and the spirit which G–d breathed into Adam was therefore part of G–d himself. According to this, we are actually activating the G–dliness within us when we speak. It is inconceivable that someone would desecrate this G–dliness by using it for something other than respectful language. Think of what you would feel like if you gave someone a gift and the next day you saw that he had put it with the trash. No doubt you would feel insulted, and rightly so. Then how must G–d feel when you take His precious gift of speech, something which is part of Himself, and soil it with indecent language!

If you speak badly about another person, you violate the prohibition against *lashon hara,* which is a grave abuse of speech. We are not privy as to what animals convey to each other, but I seriously doubt that they spread gossip. By the same token, they are not subject to listening to gossip. If that is so, then someone who speaks or listens to *lashon hara* is not only failing to elevate himself above the animal level, but even sinks beneath it.

How grievous a sin *lashon hara* is can be seen from the works of the Chafetz Chaim, who made the eradication of *lashon hara* his mission in life.

We must exercise the greatest caution to avoid *lashon hara*.

O*ne evening, after the many people who sought Rabbi Shlomo Zalman Auerbach's counsel and rulings had all left, the Rabbi sat with his wife and sister. His sister then inquired about a student in the yeshivah who was being considered as a shidduch for her daughter. "He is a fine young man," the Rabbi said.*

After a few moments the Rabbi said to his sister, "I am sure you are now going to visit our sister," who lived nearby. The sister indicated that she was indeed about to do so and left.

Upon emerging from the other sister's house, she found her brother, Rabbi Shlomo Zalman, waiting for her. "I want to tell you," he said, "that the young man you inquired about is not appropriate for your daughter."

"Then why did you not say so when I asked you in your home?" the sister asked.

Rabbi Shlomo Zalman answered, "I could not say anything uncomplimentary about this young man in the presence of my wife. Since it involves your decision about a shidduch, I am obligated to tell it to you. But for me to say it in the presence of my wife, for whom this information is not essential, would be lashon hara" (HaTorah HaMisameches).

We do not know how long Rabbi Shlomo Zalman had been standing outside waiting for his sister to emerge. We do know that he never allowed a single moment to go to waste, and every available second was spent in the study of Torah. That he could spend a period of time to give his sister the information she needed in a manner which would not transgress *lashon hara* tells us something about the gravity of this sin. This anecdote also teaches us that saying something negative about another person to one's own wife is considered *lashon hara.*

The Talmud quotes Rabbi Shimon as saying that he wished man had been created with two mouths, one of which would be uncontaminated and used only for prayer and Torah study (*Jerusalem Talmud, Berachos* 1:2). But since we have only one mouth, we must see that it remains unsoiled. Not even the finest prayer or expounding of Torah is worth much if it emanates from an unclean mouth. Would you not be repelled if the finest delicacies were served to you in a utensil that had been used for garbage?

It has truly been said that the tongue is mightier than the sword. With a sword you can kill only someone who stands close by, whereas with an unbridled tongue you can kill someone who is at the opposite end of the globe.

Obviously, killing someone is anathema to a spiritual person, and doing so with *lashon hara* should be no different.

There is often a strong temptation to abuse speech, whether in moments of rage or when one would enjoy revealing a juicy piece of gossip. This temptation must be recognized as the work of the *yetzer hara,* which will stop at nothing to obstruct man's striving for spirituality. The *yetzer hara* knows full well that it would be a waste of time to get someone to eat *tereifah,* but that we are much more vulnerable to lapses of caution in how we speak, and causing us to abuse speech therefore can become its primary mission.

R*abbi Samson Raphael Hirsch says, "The best training for faithful observance of the Torah's commandments is careful attention to our speech. There is no better way to self-perfection than the earnest resolution, the silent promise before G–d, to allow one's mouth to utter nothing devious, to keep away from unbridled prattling, never permitting his lips to move arbitrarily ... If someone's heart, therefore, is inclined to attain wisdom and obedience to the commandments, he has a ready way to train himself for that every moment of his life, through the wise use of speech" (from The Wisdom of Mishlei, page 100)*

Rabbi Hirsch continues, "The most contemptible and destructive forms of lying, however, are hypocrisy, flattery, and deceptive persuasion. Hypocrisy covers up true convictions and intentions; flattery deceives about the real character of a person; and deceptive persuasion distorts the genuine value of an action about to be carried out" (ibid.)

Let us remember Onkeles' interpretation that the gift of speech is the single most important feature that defines man, and that by abusing speech we are not only committing a serious transgression, but are also jeopardizing our very identity.

From Child to "Mentsch"

Bears, as well as many other animals, care for their young, hence we see that the parental and particularly the maternal instinct is strong in animals. The mother bear teaches her cubs how to forage for food, and when they reach the stage where they are able to find food for themselves, she leads them into the woods and then disappears. Her job as a parent is finished, and thereafter they must fend for themselves.

The human parent does not desert the child when the latter is able to survive on his own, and the trait of caring for children after they have attained the capacity to survive on their own is therefore uniquely human and is a component of spirituality,

At closer glance, the vast difference between human and animal caring for their children is more apparent than real. Inasmuch as an animal does not have a conscious ultimate purpose, and all it must do is grow in size and strength, the parental responsibility is satisfied when the young are able to find their food, which will permit them to achieve their full development.

The full development of the human child does not end with his being able to survive physically, and requires that he become a *mentsch*. The parental responsibility is therefore to provide him with all that is necessary to reach that goal. Thus, both animals and humans have a similar parental task: to give their young the means to become that which they are supposed to be. Animals have it rather easy, since they are guided in their task by instinct, which is generally infallible. Human parents cannot rely on instinct, and must give much thought to properly raising their children. Failure to do so constitutes a major defect in spirituality.

There is yet another difference between animals and man. The animal parental instinct applies to its own young, and there is no instinctual drive to care for the young of others. Judaism requires that a person look after the children of others if the parent is incapable of doing so. There is a community responsibility to provide adequate training for all children, and in absence of a parent, the task falls upon the entire community. Furthermore, when one assumes the responsibility of providing a child with Torah learning, it must be done with the same dedication as if it were one's own child.

This is what the Talmud (*Sanhedrin* 19b) means: Whoever teaches another's child Torah has the responsibility as if it were his own child.

Some parents are diligent in providing their child with the finest secular education to enable him to become a professional or enter the business world with the competence necessary for success, and they feel that by this they have satisfied their obligation. From what we have seen, providing a child with the means for sustenance is not an exclusive human trait, and limiting the child's training to this is nothing more than a more sophisticated version of an animal trait. The human parent has the obligation to provide the child with the means to become a full human being, i.e., with the means to become spiritual.

Didactic teaching is, of course, necessary. Historically, one of the first projects in any new Jewish settlement was establishing a *cheder*, and it is still the responsibility of Jewish parents to give their child full access to the lifeblood of Judaism: the Torah. However, the responsibility does not end with this. The teaching of proper *middos* (character traits) is primarily the job of the parents, not the teacher. *Middos* are taught mostly by modeling, and parents therefore have the responsibility to act and behave in a manner that will impress proper conduct and attitudes on the child. This is a lengthy subject, and I have tried to provide some guidelines in *Positive Parenting* (*Mesorah Publications*, 1996).

It is, of course, impossible to control a child's development. Solomon says "Give training to the child according to his nature" (*Proverbs* 22:6), and Rabbi

Samson Raphael Hirsch stresses the wording of the verse, that one can only give training to a child, but the child is not a piece of clay that can be molded. Whether the child accepts or rejects the training may not be up to the parents. Nevertheless, spiritual teaching should be conveyed in a manner that will be accepted by the child. Just as when the child needs a medication it is put in a pleasant tasting form so that the child will not resist taking it, so must spiritual teaching be made palatable to the child. Many failures at conveying spirituality to children are the result of compelling them to comply, rather than making spirituality pleasant tasting.

We are fortunate in having a rich heritage, with many examples of spirituality in the lives of our great Torah personalities, both men and women. Parental modeling can be enhanced by relating to children anecdotes of the lives of our great people.

Showing respect for elders and for the spiritual giants of previous generations is something which only humans can do, and this vehicle for providing proper training for our children is therefore also an aspect of spirituality.

More than Just Rest

I f one were asked to list those aspects of Judaism that are especially spiritual, one would likely list Shabbos as the foremost spiritual experience. And rightly so. Inasmuch as the goal of spirituality is to come into a closer relationship with G–d, what could possibly be as potent and strong a bond as Shabbos, of which G–d Himself stated, "Between me and the Children of Israel it (Shabbos) is an eternal sign" (*Exodus* 31:17). Shabbos is the covenant between Israel and G–d, hence it is *the* spiritual experience par excellence.

Or at least it should be. However, since we have defined spirituality as being the sum total of all the distinctions between man and animals, can we really say that a day of rest is uniquely human? Animals, too, rest when they are weary. Of course, they do not designate a particular day as a rest day, but if this is the only difference between animal rest and human rest, it is then essentially a quantitative one, hardly enough to make the day of rest the foremost spiritual experience.

The answer is that Shabbos should be far more than a day of rest. Of course, the Torah prohibits many kinds of work, and even many things which we would not classify as work. And one who refrains from doing the forbidden acts is indeed observant of the Shabbos restrictions, but a passive Shabbos falls short of the paragon of spiritual experiences.

That Shabbos is more than a day of rest is made clear by the very origin of Shabbos. "G–d blessed the seventh day and hallowed it, for on it He rested from all His work (*Genesis* 2:2). Obviously G–d was not exhausted by the work of Creation, and He designated the day of His rest as a blessed and holy day. This, then, is what Shabbos was meant to be.

Being that we are restricted from many activities and pastimes, Shabbos should be dedicated to more intensive prayer. One does not have to rush through the prayers to get to the office on time. Shabbos should be dedicated to Torah study, both individually and in groups, and in listening to the words of Torah scholars. Shabbos should be a day when parents review with their children what they have learned during the week. Shabbos should be a day when we not only abstain from work, but not even *think* of work. As the Talmud says, when Shabbos enters, all the worries of the workweek should be forgotten. Shabbos is a day when we do not even talk about anything we plan to do during the workweek.

There is a quaint custom in some families to serve "*farfel*" on Friday night, and some refer to it as "the Baal Shem's *tzimmis*." The eating of this *farfel* is accompanied by a statement which is a play on Yiddish; before we begin the dish we say, "Whatever happened until now is *farfallen*." The *farfel* is a symbolic representation of the statement — "Let bygones be bygones," and implies that on Shabbos we should cast aside all the worries we harbored during the previous week. The more we unburden ourselves of weekday worries, the more receptive our minds will be to things of *kedushah,* and we can then make the Shabbos into a truly holy day.

The mitzvah of Shabbos is contained in the Ten Commandments, and it is noteworthy that there is a difference between the wording of the Ten Commandments as they appear in *Exodus* (20:1-14) and as they appear in *Deuteronomy* (5:6-18). In *Exodus* the reason given for Shabbos is: "Because G–d created the world in six days and rested on the seventh day. Therefore G–d blessed the seventh day and hallowed it." In *Deuteronomy,* Creation is not mentioned. Instead we read: "You should remember that you were a slave in Egypt, and G–d delivered you from there. Therefore G–d commands you *to do the Shabbos.*"

The obvious question is: Why is there so marked a change in the two versions of the Ten Commandments? Furthermore, the reason of Creation is perfectly understandable. But in what way is the enslavement in Egypt related to Shabbos? Why does it not state here that G–d made the Shabbos holy? Finally, just what is meant by the command that we are "to do" the Shabbos, when Shabbos is in fact a day of "non-doing"?

With what we have said above, we can understand the two versions. The Midrash states that when Moses was a prince in Pharaoh's court, he advised Pharaoh to give the Israelite slaves a day of rest, because otherwise they would be too exhausted to do their work properly. The day chosen was the seventh day of the week, and the Israelites called it "the day of Moses." The purpose of this day of rest was therefore for the slaves to recharge their batteries so that they could work more efficiently during the next week. The day of rest was thus subordinate to the workweek.

When G–d gave the Children of Israel the Ten Commandments, the reason He gave for Shabbos was because He rested on the seventh day of Creation, and as we noted, this had nothing to do with exhaustion. Rather, Shabbos was the most important day of the week, and it was blessed and holy. In the desert, where the Israelites' food was the manna from heaven, where the well of Miriam provided all the water they needed, where their clothes and shoes grew right along with them, where they were sheltered from the elements by the Clouds of Glory, the Israelites did not need to rest from the exhaustion of the workweek, and it was clear that Shabbos was to be a sacred day.

The Ten Commandments were repeated by Moses in *Deuteronomy*, at a time when the Israelites stood at the threshold of Canaan. Once they would enter the holy land, they would no longer have manna or the well of

Miriam. There would be no protective Clouds of Glory, and clothes would have to be replaced when they wore out or when they were outgrown. In order to get food, they would have to till the fields, sow, fertilize, harvest, winnow, grind, and bake. They would have to dig many wells for water. They would have to construct or maintain houses for shelter, and they would have to shear the sheep, spin the wool, and sew clothes. There would be a workweek at the end of which one might indeed be exhausted and wish to rest.

This kind of a Shabbos would be similar to the day of rest in Egypt, and Moses wished to instruct the Israelites that they should not observe a day of rest that was appropriate for slaves. G–d had delivered them from slavery, and they were now a "kingdom of priests and a sacred nation" (*Exodus* 19:6). Moses therefore told them: "You may remember the enslavement in Egypt and the day of rest you had there, a totally passive day of rest. This is *not* the kind of Shabbos you are to observe. Rather, G–d wishes you '*to do*' the Shabbos; i.e. to engage in spiritual pursuits on Shabbos in accordance with its holiness."

The two versions of the mitzvah of Shabbos are now understandable. The first is the mitzvah of how one *should* observe Shabbos, while the second is a warning not to regress to the passive day of rest of Egypt which was subordinate to the workweek, and Moses alerted the Israelites that this was *not* the way Shabbos was meant to be observed.

Shabbos was blessed and hallowed by G–d, but we must partake of its blessing and of its holiness, for only then is Shabbos the full spiritual experience.

Unselfish Prayer

2 6

e noted earlier that prayer is not unique to humans, because the Scriptures state that other living things look to G–d for their sustenance, as, for example, "He gives food to the animals, to the young of the ravens when they call to Him" (*Psalms* 147:9); or, "The young lions roar for prey, and ask G–d for their food" (ibid. 104:21); or, "They all (the creatures) hope to You, that You will give them their food in its time" (ibid. v. 27). However, all these prayers are for the animals' own needs, and there is no indication that they can pray for other than themselves. Prayer for others is therefore uniquely human, and when we pray for others, we are spiritual.

The Talmud gives high praise for those who pray for others (*Bava Kamma* 92a) and censures Noah, who saved himself from the flood, but did not pray for others to be saved. Abraham, on the other hand, even prayed for mercy for a decadent population, and Moses repeatedly pleaded for forgiveness for the Israelites.

Praying for others is in line with other benevolent centrifugal actions, and those who feel most for others and intercede on their behalf are highly spiritual. My great-grandfather, the Rabbi of Hornostipol, said that a person's prayers will be answered if what he asks for is indeed what he wants most. People think that certain things are their most intense desire, but they are deceiving themselves. For example, a person may say that he has an intense desire for wealth, but if his head were held under water he would hardly desire wealth, because his desire would be to be able to breathe air. The reason why the prayers of *tzaddikim* were effective is because when they prayed for others, their *ahavas Yisrael* was so intense and all-absorbing, that if you had held their head under water, they would still have thought of the other's needs rather than the need of filling their lungs with air to save their lives. This sounds beyond human capacity, but it is possible for those who have achieved an absolute self-effacement and live only for others. We may not aspire to that dazzling height of spirituality, but at least it gives us a taste of what our concern for others should be.

My great-grandfather, the Rebbe of Hornostipol, had a large following of devotees. He suffered from a heart condition which ultimately took his life in his early 60s.

One time, great-grandfather developed a severe bout of hiccups, which stubbornly refused to respond to every known remedy. After three days of unabated hiccuping, it was feared that his heart might be affected, and he was advised to consult a neurologist in Kiev.

Accompanied by his gabbai (attendant), who also served as interpreter since the Rebbe knew little Russian, he went to Kiev. After completing the examination, the professor said that the only way to rid him of the hiccups was to deliver a shock to the spinal cord. This was accomplished by applying a red-hot poker to the spinal column.

The gabbai interpreted the doctor's message, to which great-grandfather responded with, "Nu," and proceeded to strip to the waist. The doctor put a poker into the fire, and after it reached a glowing heat, he ran it down the spinal column. Great-grandfather did not flinch a muscle nor emit a sound.

The doctor was bewildered. He saw the searing mark of the burn, yet the lack of any reaction made him think that the treatment did not "take." He reheated the poker, and again applied it down the spinal column, this time with greater pressure. Again, not a whimper from the patient.

The doctor threw the poker into the fireplace and exclaimed, " I cannot understand this! This is *not a human being; this is some kind of angel. Why, the other day I was ready to perform this very treatment on a robust, husky Cossack, and no sooner did I remove the poker from the fire than he jumped out the second-floor window. Here I have seared this man twice, and he does not even move a muscle!"*

Great-grandfather asked the gabbai, "What did the doctor say?" and the gabbai translated the doctor's comment.

Great-grandfather only sighed. "You know," he said, "when someone comes to me for help, and in spite of how much I wish to help him, there is nothing I can do, and if at such a time I do not jump out the window from anguish, I certainly do not have to do so now."

In chassidic writings it is stressed that the finest prayer is when one prays for the glory of G–d to be revealed, as is said: "Not for us, G–d, but for the honor of Your Name" (*Psalms* 115:1). When Jews are oppressed, nations of the world may jeer, "Where is their G–d?" Therefore, "Come to our salvation to preserve Your honor."

The Talmud says that when Jews suffer, G–d feels their pain, and that when a person is in distress, he should pray for relief so that G–d will not have to suffer along with him. We are told that G–d wept when he had to punish Israel for its sins and drive them into exile (*Chagigah* 5b), and our prayers for return to our homeland and the rebuilding of the Temple should be to alleviate the Divine distress. Unselfish prayers, whether they be for others or for G–d, are the prayers of highly spiritual people,

The *tzaddik* of Sanz used to relate a parable before the High Holidays.

A young prince committed offenses for which he was sent into exile in the farthest corner of the king's realm. Not having learned any skills in the palace, the prince had great difficulty in supporting himself, failing at whatever he tried. He then decided to be a shepherd, because watching over a flock required no special skills.

The prince noticed that other shepherds had built themselves little thatched huts to protect them from the heat of the sun. But alas! Every time he tried to construct such a hut it fell apart, and he remained beneath the merciless rays of the sun.

One day the prince overheard that the king was soon to visit a nearby city, and that there was a custom to write brief petitions and throw them into the royal coach during the king's parade through the streets. The king would read whatever petitions fell into the royal coach, and grant the request. The prince then wrote a petition that he be given help to construct a hut to protect him from the sun, joined the crowd lining the streets, and succeeded in throwing his petition into the royal coach. Recognizing his son's writing, the king burst into tears. "How terribly low my son has sunk, that he has completely forgotten that he is a prince, and all he aspires to is a thatched hut! Why, his petition should have been to be returned to the palace, where he could again live the life of a prince!"

As he told the parable, the tzaddik of Sanz would weep along with the king. "Soon we will have Rosh Hashanah and Yom Kippur, days that are propitious for our prayers to be answered. What do we ask for? Only our mundane needs, comparable to the prince's request for a thatched hut. Our prayers should be for G–d to return us to our homeland and to the glory of the Israel of old. How it must pain G–d to see that we have drifted so far away from Him that we do not even aspire to be returned to His Temple in Jerusalem."

Yes, had the prince requested that he be forgiven and brought back to the royal court his prayer would have been selfish, but it would have indicated an appreciation of what it meant to him to be close to his father, the king, once again.

Our prayers, whether for others, for G–d, or even for ourselves in the sense of asking to be restored to the palace of our Father, the King, are uniquely human, and when we pray this way, we are spiritual.

The Hebrew word for prayer, *tefillah,* is related to the term "to bind" (see *Rashi, Genesis* 30:8). When we pray to G–d, we relate to Him, and each time we do so with *kavanah* we are brought closer to Him. When we ask G–d for our needs or express our gratitude, we increase our awareness of our total dependence on Him and we cling to Him for dear life, much as an infant clings to a parent. When we praise G–d, our reverence and love for Him is increased. Thus, prayer brings us closer to G–d in many ways.

The Talmud states that the reason why the matriarchs Sarah and Rebecca were childless for many years is because G–d favors the intense prayers of *tzaddikim* (*Yevamos* 64a). How foolish it would be to think that G–d would deprive these righteous women of children for selfish reasons, just because he wishes to hear their prayers. What the Talmud means is that intense prayer enhances one's spirituality, and inasmuch as the matriarchs were to be the mothers of *klal Yisrael* (the entire congregation of Israel), it was necessary that they be at the highest level of spirituality, and this could only come about through their praying intensely for what was dearest to them.

There is a rather unusual expression where Kind David says, "I am a prayer" (*Psalms* 109:4). One of the commentaries explains that if a person rings your doorbell, and he appears well fed and neatly dressed, you have no idea what he wants until he tells you. However, if the person appears gaunt and in tattered clothes, he does not have to say anything. His very appearance bespeaks his needs.

In spite of his being a king, David's humility was profound, as he says: "I am but a worm, and not even a man" (ibid. 22:7). David felt he was so needy spiritually that anyone who looked at him would promptly detect this. Hence he says to G–d, "I do not have to say anything. My spiritual needs are self-evident. My very being constitutes a prayer."

David was confident that G–d hears his prayers, and that was sufficient reason for him to declare, "Serve G–d with joy, come before Him with song" (ibid. 100:2). Prayer should therefore be not only with *kavanah*, but also with *simchah,* because we should rejoice in being brought ever closer to G–d.

The Positive Extinguishes the Negative

P rayer also has a very powerful component which is often underutilized.

How often were you sitting and reading something which required concentration, when suddenly there was the shrill noise of a screaming siren that pierced your ears and disturbed your concentration? How often were you relaxing or beginning to doze off when the combined wailing and foghorn sounds of an emergency vehicle interrupted your rest, and perhaps even caused sufficient agitation so that you could not get back to your relaxed state?

There is a way to lessen this irritation. When the vehicle is either an ambulance or rescue squad, a fire engine, or a police car, all of which are responding to some trouble, what if, upon hearing the siren, you uttered a brief prayer: "Dear G–d, if that is an ambulance or rescue squad, please have it reach the patient or hospital in time to save the person's life. If it is a fire engine, please have it reach the building in time to save it. And if it is a police car, let them get to the scene before any harm is done."

Just as light banishes darkness, so do good thoughts banish bad thoughts, and consideration banishes irritation. When you think or verbalize this brief prayer, you will find yourself much less affected by the sirens.

Incidentally, there have been some fascinating studies that have demonstrated that patients for whom people prayed had more complete recoveries, *even though they had no idea that someone was praying for them!* How can this be explained scientifically? I don't know. I am just reporting research which has been substantiated. Do you realize how good you will feel knowing that your prayer may be benefiting someone? This is at least as potent a relaxing agent as a tranquilizer, and has no undesirable side effects.

But let's go further. If this becomes widespread, as it should, then the patient who is being transported to the hospital will know that the siren will alert countless people to pray for him. The fire fighters and police will feel strengthened and encouraged by the knowledge that many people are pulling for them and praying for their safety and success.

L*et me share with you just one personal experience which demonstrates the power of prayer.*

As an intern, I was called to administer an intra-venous medication to a patient. His nurse told me that he had been undergoing orthopedic surgery when he had had a sudden cardiac arrest, and the surgeon immediately cut open his chest and manually massaged the heart, which responded well. When the patient awoke with bandages on his chest and learned that he had suffered a cardiac arrest he became very depressed, and was not responding well to his treatment.

After I administered the medication, the patient said, "Are you a Rabbi?" "Yes," I said. He then continued, "I am not Jewish, but can you say a prayer with me?" "Of course," I said.

I then began thinking what prayer would be familiar to both of us, and I thought that psalm 23 is generally well known. I began reciting the psalm, and the patient joined me. When we came to the verse, "Yea, though I walk in the valley of the shadow of death, I will fear no evil because Thou art with me," the patient paused and his eyes welled up with tears. When we finished the psalm, he thanked me profusely.

The next day the nurse told me that there had been a miraculous change in the patient's demeanor, and when I entered the room he was sitting upright and greeted me with a wide smile, "Hi there, Doc." He then said, "When I found out that my heart had stopped, I realized that if it could happen once, it could happen again, but this time there might not be anyone around to get it started again. I was afraid of dying. But when we read the psalm about not being afraid when walking in the shadow of death because G–d is there, I realized that this was about me! When my heart stopped I was dead, but thank G–d, He gave me more life.

"I am a retired police sergeant, and I worked honestly all my life. I think that I have done enough good in my lifetime, that I walked with G–d, and I can expect that when I die, He will walk with me. Who knows? I may live ten more years or I may die tomorrow, but I am no longer afraid."

The patient then shook my hand and said, "Thanks, Doc. That prayer sure beat the daylights out of that medication."

Yes, the power of prayer is immeasurable. And when you pray at the sound of a siren, you are doing someone a great favor, which is a good feeling. You cannot feel both good and bad at the same time. The positive extinguishes the negative.

Diligence

hile on a speaking engagement in South Africa, I had the opportunity to go on safari in the African jungle. The guide told me that if I wished to see any of the animals, I must rise at dawn when they go to their watering places, because after they had hunted for their food and quenched their thirst, they generally did not roam around, and just lolled about in the sun. It would be wrong to refer to these animals as being indolent, because there is nothing that they should be doing in which they are derelict. *Diligence* is not an animal trait.

But human beings do have the capacity to be diligent. Over and above caring for our physical needs, which is a characteristic we share with animals, we can set both proper short-term and long-term goals for ourselves, and strive to fulfill them diligently. Indeed, how much we value the goals we have set can be measured by how diligent we are in their pursuit.

Some people are chronic procrastinators, but they can act very swiftly and with diligence to get something they really want. The things that a procrastinator postpones are those which do not interest him very much and which he would rather avoid altogether if that were possible.

As we have noted, the proper goal in Judaism is to develop a close relationship with G–d by fulfilling His mitzvos. A person may fulfill mitzvos because he feels compelled to do so but considers them burdensome, or he may do so because his love for G–d motivates him to seek an ever closer relationship with Him. The two can be distinguished by the degree of diligence with which one performs mitzvos. The greatness of the patriarch Abraham and his intense love for G–d is evidenced not only by his willingness to sacrifice his own child if that were G–d's will, but even more so by the fact that he arose early in the morning to do so. It would have been perfectly understandable if Abraham had delayed this formidable challenge in order to spend a few extra hours with his beloved son. His diligence in wishing to do the Divine will as soon as possible testifies to his intense love for G–d.

We may make a pledge for *tzedakah*, but repeatedly delay remitting it. A true appreciation of the mitzvah of *tzedakah* would result in prompt payment. Perhaps many of us feel that we are fulfilling the mitzvah of *tefill-in* properly when we put them on in the morning, but few of us are like Rabbi Levi Yitzchak of Berditchev, who sat by the window all night after the last day of Passover and Succos, looking for the first sign of dawn, which would enable him to fulfill the mitzvah of *tefillin,* a mitzvah which he could not perform during the festival.

The opposite of diligence is *indolence,* and Solomon goes to great length to emphasize the destructive nature of indolence.

I passed by the field of a lazy man,
and by the vineyard of a man devoid of understanding,
and I saw everything come up in thistles;
the surface was covered with thorns;
and the stone wall was torn down.
This I saw and set my heart to it,
I saw it and learned the lesson:
Yet a little sleep, a little slumber,
a little folding of the hands to rest,
and your poverty will stalk you,
and your wants will come upon you as an armed man.
(Proverbs 24:30-34).

Solomon describes both the behavior of the lazy man and its inevitable consequences. In other passages, Solomon uses the Hebrew word *remiyah* to refer to indolence (*Proverbs* 10:4; 12:24; 19:15). *Remiyah* means deceit or betrayal, and Rabbi Samson Raphael Hirsch explains that the indolent person, by failing to use the powers given to him for the true ultimate purpose is committing deceit, and is betraying G–d Who has given him that strength (*The Wisdom of Mishlei,* page 164).

Solomon also gives an accurate description of the rationalizations which the indolent person uses to justify his failure to act.

The lazy man says: There is a jackal in the way,
a lion in the streets.
The door is already turning on its hinges,
and the sluggard is still in bed.
The sluggard already puts his hand on the plate,
but is too lazy to bring it to his mouth.
The lazy man thinks himself wiser
then seven sensible counselors.
(Proverbs 26:13-16).

The rationalizations offered by the lazy person may be patently ridiculous, yet he thinks himself wise in his dereliction. It should also be noted that the lazy person may begin with just a touch of indolence, "yet a little sleep, a little slumber," but the indolence may rapidly accelerate and intensify to result in impoverishment.

It may take considerable energy to overcome indolence, because the natural state of all matter is *inertia*. This explains the Midrash which states that over every blade of grass there stands an angel which commands it, "Grow!" (*Bereishis Rabbah* 10:7). We might ask why this is necessary. Given that there is the seed, fertile soil, and abundant water, it is only natural that the grass will grow. The answer is that even with all the necessary ingredients available, matter would remain in a lifeless state of inertia if it were not forced to change.

Man, too, has the inertia that is characteristic of all matter, and an expenditure of energy is required to overcome this inertia. The indolent person will not put forth the requisite effort, and the seed that could develop into greatness may lie dormant forever.

Diligence is the badge of a spiritual person.

Pursuit of
Thrills

I t is difficult to determine whether other living things seek to have thrills. Certainly when we see monkeys leaping and swinging gracefully from vine to vine, it appears that this may be a thrilling feat for them. On the other hand, to them it may be as commonplace as walking is for us. But even if animals do go for thrills, they do not have an entire industry dedicated to thrill seeking the way humans do, and we may therefore classify this kind of thrill-seeking as uniquely human.

When we discussed truth and falsehood, we concluded that although animals do not lie, the unique human capacity of lying is a feature of spirituality only when one *overcomes* the impulse to lie. We may have to look at thrill seeking in a somewhat similar light.

Having grown up in America and experienced the thrill of baseball and football, I can hardly condemn those who are rabid sports fans. However, if we wish to take a serious look at spirituality, we must look critically at sports and other thrills.

Sports generally consist of an activity that presents a challenge, and there is a thrill when that challenge is mastered. Thus, the pitcher challenges the batter to hit the ball, and the batter triumphs when he hits the ball in such a manner that none of the defensive players can catch it. If he puts it beyond the reach of all the defensive players, he has achieved the ultimate triumph by hitting a home run. Inasmuch as most of us are not adept at performing in this way, we may achieve thrills by proxy, by becoming a fan of that team and essentially identifying with the athlete and thereby sharing in his thrill.

All well and good, but what has this triumph produced other than a thrill? There is no product that anyone can put to use in any way. The triumphs of medical science produce lifesaving treatments, and the triumphs of technology produce computers, automobiles, jet planes, air conditioners, and other products that can be put to use. But no product results from even a dramatic game-saving grand slam, and all we are left with is a thrill.

Most of the activities that are compensated are those that produce a useful product. If, for example, a tailor would offer to stitch all day, but never produce anything that could be used as a garment, there would hardly be any reason to compensate him for pointless sewing. Indeed, work that does not result in a product would not be tolerable even if it were compensated.

It is related that a wealthy man saw a peasant harvesting grain, cutting the stalks with a scythe. "How much are you paid for this work?" he asked. "Sixty *kopecks* a day plus a shot of vodka," the peasant answered. "Come work for me," the man said, "and I will pay you 120 *kopecks* a day plus two shots of vodka." The peasant readily agreed, and accompanied the man to his home.

The man took the peasant into an empty room and said, "Your assignment is to make the same motions with the scythe that you did in the field." The peasant began swinging the scythe as if he were cutting grain, but after an hour told the man he was quitting. "I will pay you even more," the man said. "*Nyet,*" the peasant said. "But why?" the man asked. "Because," the peasant said, "I am accomplishing nothing by waving my scythe in the air, and I can't stand it."

Obviously, there is something in human nature that makes a purposeless activity intolerable, at least over the long run.

Western civilization has a concept of "fun." An analysis of "fun" reveals it to often be an activity which accomplishes nothing tangible. In fact, if someone is asked why he is doing something and responds, "For the fun of it," it means that the activity does not result in any useful product or service. It is of interest that neither in

Hebrew nor in Yiddish is there a word equivalent to the English "fun." There are words for pleasure, play, and amusement, but not for "fun." This indicates that the concept of a meaningless activity is alien to Judaism.

This does not mean that one may not enjoy engaging in or watching sports, but it does mean that we have to recognize it for what it is. If our emotional and mental health is enhanced by the thrill of sports, then it may serve a purpose. However, just as too much salt or sugar can ruin a tasty dish, so can excessive amounts of time spent on "fun" be detrimental.

Except for a judicious dose of "fun," which is far less than some people seek, our thrills should come from Torah and mitzvos. If we truly believe that Torah and mitzvos are the ultimate goal and the reason for which we were created, and that there is a major challenge to overcome because a very powerful *yetzer hara* uses every trick in the book to deter us from Torah and mitzvos, then learning and observing the latter can provide a very substantial thrill.

Let us realize that winning the struggle with the *yetzer hara* is overcoming a real challenge that exists in the world. Home runs and touchdowns may be fun, but the challenges of hitting the ball over the fence or running the ball into the end zone did not exist until we devised them by building ball parks and football fields. In other words, these are really man-made challenges, which we have set up only to overcome them. With all due respect to sports devotees, this is not much different than a child who builds a tall column for the sole purpose of having the thrill of knocking it down.

As the Baal Shem Tov said, spirituality does not necessarily mean divesting ourselves of certain traits, but rather redirecting them and channeling them toward more appropriate goals. This is true of the desire for thrills. If animals do have such a desire, there is nothing they can do other than to gratify it in the only way they know. A human being can utilize the impulse for thrill-seeking to experience thrills in study of Torah and performance of mitzvos. A Torah scholar will tell you that there is an exquisite thrill in reconciling an apparent conflict of two rulings by the Rambam, and someone who has done an act of *chesed* and knows that he has been of substantial help to another person can tell you what a thrill that is. What we must do is to expand upon these, so that we receive most of our thrills from something that is truly meaningful rather than from creating challenges just so that we may overcome them, which in the final analysis is nothing but pointless fun.

The spiritual person wishes to put every available moment to good use, and he will therefore try to get his thrills from activities that are truly meaningful.

Grief vs. Mourning

Are grief and mourning identical?

Grief is a sensation, a painful sensation at having lost something precious. One may grieve over the loss of a loved one, and may also grieve over other kinds of losses. There is little doubt that many creatures experience what we can only interpret as grief. Doves may lose apparent interest in life after a mate dies, and dogs have been known to pine away after their master died.

Mourning, however, is something else. Mourning is more of an intellectual rather than an affective experience. One may *grieve* over the loss of a relative or friend, but *mourn* the family's or community's loss of what that person could have provided by his love, care, and guidance. Mourning is more of a sign of admiration and respect for the person, and an acknowledgment that his contributions to the family or society were indeed appreciated. It is customary that when a person who was a benefactor to society or a prominent government official dies, the community or country proclaims a period of *mourning*, which may be observed by people who are not emotionally affected by his death. While animals may *grieve*, it is doubtful that they can *mourn*.

Each year on Tishah B'Av we mourn the loss of the Temple in Jerusalem, an event which occurred more than 2,000 years ago. While some people may actually grieve and feel pain over this loss, most Jews simply comply with the *halachos* of mourning on Tishah B'Av. It is self-evident that while *halachah* can prescribe the manner by which one should mourn — fasting, not wearing shoes, sitting on the ground, etc. — *halachah* cannot legislate how one should feel.

People who have achieved a high level of spirituality, and who understand the loss of spirituality that resulted from the destruction of the Temple, may actually feel the pain, and they may grieve as well as mourn.

How much we mourn the loss of a source of spirituality may be a measure of how far we are advanced in spirituality. For example, the portion of the Torah read on Yom Kippur begins with the death of the two sons of Aaron, the High Priest. In many *machzorim* (holiday prayer books) there is a note that if one sheds tears for the death of the two sons of Aaron, he will be rewarded. Rabbi Chaim Shmuleviz asks: Is it reasonable to be moved to tears by a tragedy that occurred 3,000 years ago? He goes on to explain that the two sons of Aaron, Nadav and Avihu, were extraordinarily great people of Torah wisdom, and in fact are considered on a par with Moses. Had they not died prematurely, they would certainly have contributed a great deal to Torah knowledge, and their early death deprived us of this. A person who values Torah and has an insatiable thirst for Torah knowledge can appreciate what their loss has meant to Judaism, and if he feels this to the point that he is moved to tears, he is indeed to be rewarded for attaining an exceptionally high level of spirituality.

This is also why the Talmud has harsh words for someone who does not participate in mourning the death of a Torah scholar, because this indicates a lack of understanding of the significance of Torah knowledge for our lives.

From the time of the Talmud to our very own day, students and followers of a Torah scholar have taken the teacher's death as a deep personal loss. Rabbi Akiva could not be consoled when his master, Rabbi Eliezer, died. When Rabbi Shimon ben Lakish died, his teacher Rabbi Yochanan, who ultimately became his colleague, mourned his death so intensely that he soon died. In our own generation, people who were with the Steipler Gaon on the Shabbos that the Chazon Ish died were surprised that the Steipler showed no signs of mourning. No sooner had Shabbos come to a close when the Steipler wept bitterly. This *tzaddik* was able to restrain himself from manifesting his grief on Shabbos, but when Shabbos was over, his profound grief at the loss of this Torah luminary overwhelmed him and he could not find solace.

We have already noted the importance of *simchah* upon doing a mitzvah. Just as such *simchah* indicates our awareness that mitzvos bring us closer to G–d, similarly, mourning the loss of any source of Torah knowledge indicates that we are aware of having lost something that would have facilitated our bonding with G–d.

In addition to being a spiritual trait, mourning actually enhances spirituality. As we have noted, grief is a natural phenomenon, but it is also an emotion which can impair a person's function by rendering him sleepless, depressing his appetite, and draining his energies and interest in life. In addition, no two people can live in a close relationship without ever having their differences, and when one dies, the survivor may have guilt feelings as he recalls their disagreements. The rituals of mourning, the *shivah*, the thirty days, and the twelve-month observance for the death of a parent help dissipate the grief as one ventilates one's feelings, and as one conducts himself in the manner that the Talmud tells us is beneficial to the *neshamah* of the departed. As the grief is dissipated, one can return to the important business of leading a normal life and pursuing the goals of spirituality.

For the spiritual person, life has great value, and each day is an opportunity to grow. When grief occurs, it must not be allowed to derail a person or render him inactive. By dissipating grief, mourning relieves its paralytic effect. By truly appreciating the spiritual as well as personal loss resulting from a death, the survivor may be stimulated to compensate for the loss by increasing his own spirituality.

Appreciation of
Nature

Q uite probably animals have an appreciation of nature at some level, but they
cannot possibly appreciate the grandeur of
nature the way man can. The importance of appreciation of nature in
spirituality can be seen in Rambam, who states that the
way a person can come to reverence and love of G–d is
through recognizing His enormous wisdom as contained
in nature (*Yesodei HaTorah* 2:2).

We may walk past trees that have thousands of
leaves and give no thought to the miracle of photosyn-
thesis and to the incomparable engineering in the

structure of a leaf. One does not have to travel to Niagara Falls to have a breathtaking experience. All one needs to do is look intelligently through a microscope at a simple leaf.

I sometimes wonder: How was it possible for the Israelites, who had witnessed unprecedented miracles in Egypt followed by the parting of the waters of the Red Sea, to have any doubts about G–d providing for them in the desert, as Scripture relates? I believe it was because they were so accustomed to so many miraculous happenings that they related to miracles the way we relate to nature, and since they did not perceive them as miracles but as natural events, they did not know how there could be food and water in a barren desert. "Our ancestors in Egypt did not understand Your wonders, and therefore did not remember Your abundant kindnesses" (*Psalms* 106:6). Anything that occurs with regularity or is commonplace loses its impact, and that is why we are derelict in recognizing the miracles within nature.

To anyone who has studied physiology, the human body is a virtually unbelievable organism. If one were to try to duplicate the functions of the liver, it is doubtful that a fully computerized four-story laboratory could accomplish the myriad of chemical and enzymatic processes with anywhere near the precision of the four pound liver. And if one would study the central nervous system, one would discover that in the brain there are over *14 billion units* (cells), all multiply interconnected, which process all the incoming data from our senses of vision, hearing, touch, smell, and taste, and send messages to the appropriate body organs and limbs, with perhaps millions of interactions occurring every minute. The one pound organ that resides within the human skull makes the Internet system appear like a simple tinker-toy by comparison. And at the base of the brain there is a gland no larger than a thumbnail, which constantly analyzes the chemical composition of the blood, especially the various hormones and mineral levels, and regulates it with an uncanny precision by sending messages to the appropriate glands and organs. This refers only to the brain itself; we know very little about the actual function of the *human mind*, which although intimately associated with the brain, is not accessible to examination via a microscope. Any person with intelligence would stand in awe at this and other marvelous works in nature, and indeed come to a reverence for G–d. And the realization of what G–d has provided for us in nature would lead to the love of G–d, as Rambam says.

It is a mitzvah to recite *Tehillim* (*Psalms*) and it is a mitzvah to study *Tehillim*. But if one wishes to appreciate the adoration of G–d through nature, let him read psalm 104 carefully.

The importance of appreciating nature is further made evident where King David cites the virtues of Torah: "The Torah of G–d is perfect, restoring the soul; the testimony of G–d is trustworthy, making the simple one wise, etc." (*Psalms* 19:8-10). However, he precedes his praise of Torah with: "The heavens declare the glory of G–d, and the expanse of the sky tells of His handiwork etc." (ibid. vs. 2-7). If one thinks of the infinite greatness and wisdom of G–d as testified to by nature, one can approach the Torah with greater respect and admiration.

The concept of the Rambam is further proven by the fact that prior to our reciting the *Shema*, in which we declare our loyalty to and love for G–d, the sages composed a lengthy *berachah* which extols the greatness of G–d as seen in nature, and draws upon psalm 104: "How great are Your works, O G–d, You make them all with wisdom, the world is full of Your possessions" (ibid. 104:24).

Only a human being has the capacity to see the greatness of G–d in nature, and when we do so, we are being spiritual.

32
Serving for Reward

hen we read: "Do not be like servants who serve the master in order to receive reward, but be like servants who serve the master without intent to receive reward" (*Ethics of the Fathers* 1:3), we may think, "That is too high a level of spirituality for us to aspire to, and it is more than adequate if we will observe Torah and mitzvos for the sake of reward."

At least, that is the way I felt, until I observed some of the performances of dolphins and walruses at the Seaquarium. These animals followed the instructions of the trainer and performed fascinating stunts, and upon completion of each stunt they received a fish. I then realized that this is also how we train mice in the laboratory to push certain levers: We give them a food pellet each time they do what we want. It then occurred to me that if I follow G-d's commandments because I want to be rewarded, I am really not acting above an animal level, and I am too proud for that. Granted that the fish reward for the dolphins is both immediate and tangible, whereas the reward I expect is long delayed and intangible, but that is not enough to satisfy my ego. Serving for reward is demeaning.

Of course, nothing more can be expected of dolphins. Although they seem to be quite intelligent animals, they are incapable of conceptualizing that there is an inherent good in an act, and then performing it because doing good is right and proper. Consequently, the only motivation they have is to receive a reward. But inasmuch as I have the intelligence to realize that a good act should be done for its own sake, I should be motivated by this principle rather than by something that I share with lower forms of life. I therefore concluded that what we are instructed in *Ethics of the Fathers* is not at all intended for people of exceptionally high spirituality, but to the contrary, it is elementary spirituality to be qualitatively different than animals.

There are pitfalls in serving G-d primarily for reward. It is conceivable that a person may think that the pleasure he will get from a behavior forbidden by the Torah offsets any reward, and if reward is his primary motivation, he may do what he feels is to his greatest advantage. We have noted earlier that our judgment processes are very susceptible to distortion by personal interest, and we may easily rationalize why we may do something that pleases us. It is therefore fundamental to Torah observance that we do what is right because it is right, and desist from wrong because it is wrong, rather than because of reward or punishment.

It is related that one Succos there was a dearth of esrogim (citrons), and the Gaon of Vilna was extremely distressed that he might not be able to fulfill the mitzvah of the four species. On the day before Succos he asked his students to find out whether anyone in Vilna had been able to procure an esrog, and to offer whatever price he would request.

One student did find that a very wealthy citizen of Vilna had an esrog, but the man was not willing to part with it for any amount of money. In desperation, the student said, "If you will sell this esrog to the Gaon, I promise you that the reward for the mitzvah will belong to you." Upon hearing this offer, the man promptly gave him the esrog.

When the Gaon saw the esrog, his joy was boundless. The student was hesitant to tell the Gaon about the promise he had made in order to obtain the esrog, but when the Gaon asked how he had managed to get it, he had no choice other than to admit the truth, expecting to be sharply reprimanded. Instead, the Gaon's joy increased and he said, "Although I have not been *motivated to do mitzvos for reward, I could not escape the fact that in the back of my mind I knew that I would be rewarded, and my intentions to do the mitzvah solely because it was the will of G-d could not be completely pure. But now that I know that the reward for this mitzvah will not be mine, I will finally have the opportunity to do a mitzvah solely because it is G-d's will, unblemished by even the slightest consideration of reward."*

Children who have not reached the age of reason must be "bribed" to do good by offering them candy or some other prize. This should be beneath the dignity of a mature, intelligent person.

In this light we may better understand the episode which relates that the patriarch Isaac told his son, Esau, to hunt food for him, whereupon he would give him his blessing (*Genesis* 27:1-46). Allegedly, Esau was Isaac's favorite, whereas Rebecca preferred Jacob. Rebecca then prevailed upon Jacob to pose as Esau and obtain Isaac's blessings for himself, and Jacob reluctantly did his mother's bidding. When Isaac discovered the ruse, he was shaken to the point where "he felt that Gehinnom had opened beneath him (*Rashi, ibid.* 27:33).

How are we to understand this? Is it conceivable that the saintly patriarch Isaac was duped to prefer the profligate Esau over the sincere Jacob? And what was so horrible about giving the blessing to Jacob that he felt that "Gehinnom had opened beneath him"?

Let us assume what was undoubtedly correct, that Isaac was well aware that Jacob was virtuous and spiritual, and that Esau was a degenerate. Isaac knew that it was the Divine wish that he bring about the birth of the Jewish people, and that it was Jacob whose spirituality made him worthy of being the father of the chosen people.

However, Isaac did not wish to give up hope of salvaging Esau. He knew that Esau was not about to be swayed by the lofty ideal of doing what is right solely because it is right, but perhaps he could be enticed by the more primitive and juvenile desire to do something for the sake of getting a "prize." He therefore said to Esau, "Look, my son. It is a great mitzvah to do things for parents. Go bring me some food, and in return for this you will get a valuable blessing. That can be a precedent for you, for when you will do good deeds, you will receive a reward."

Isaac was secure that Jacob was dedicated to doing what was right for its own sake, but knowing that he could not expect this of Esau, he tried to convince him that good deeds would be rewarded, and perhaps this might succeed in getting Esau to abandon his decadent behavior.

When Isaac discovered that Jacob had come for the blessing, and not knowing that he had been compelled to do so by his mother, his entire world was shattered. He knew that Esau was a degenerate whom he had hoped to reclaim with the juvenile concept of rewarding good deeds. But that Jacob would stoop so low as to ask for reward for a mitzvah was something that he never thought possible. Indeed he felt that "Gehinnom had opened beneath him," because Esau was almost hopeless, and if Jacob was motivated by reward, then he was not much better. Who then would carry out the Divine will of bringing the Jewish nation into being?

Of course we know that this was not what Jacob was thinking at all, and his motivations were absolutely proper.

The dolphins who perform stunts at the trainer's commands are not doing so to please the trainer. It is the fish they want, and they are essentially serving themselves.

We have noted that the characteristic of a spiritual person is that his motivations are centrifugal rather than centripetal. It is therefore basic and elementary spirituality to "be like a servant who serves the master without the intent of receiving reward."

To Be Truly Free

Earlier we noted that humans have the capacity to delay gratification, whereas animals lack this trait. As we have noted, a person may have a strong desire to do something which is completely appropriate — say, take a luxury cruise — and may have the money to do so, but because he has a number of obligations or for other reasons, he decides to postpone his excursion until a more propitious time, which may be weeks or months away. The capacity to postpone is uniquely human, because an animal does whatever it desires when the desire occurs.

In general, animals are not free to make decisions,

because they are at the mercy of their bodily impulses. If an animal is hungry, it is driven to look for food and must do so. An animal cannot decide not to eat when it is hungry. It is inconceivable that an animal will decide, "I am going to fast today." This is equally true of all other physical impulses which totally dominate an animal's behavior. Man is alone in being able to resist a bodily urge, and deny himself gratification of a strong desire if he considers it to be inappropriate.

Some philosophers deny that man has freedom of choice, and contend that a person has a number of impulses and ideas, some of which are in conflict, and that his behavior is determined by whichever impulse or idea happens to be the strongest. They say that because man is aware of the struggle within himself he has an illusion that he is making a choice, whereas the choice is really being made for him. Judaism categorically rejects this concept which, by denying free will, essentially reduces man to an animal level, with the only distinguishing feature being that man is conscious of the struggle between the opposing forces within him. Freedom of choice is a fundamental axiom of Judaism. In fact, Judaism teaches that although G–d is in control of everything in the universe, He has divested himself of control over man's decisions, and does not intervene in man's moral or ethical choices.

The idea that the strongest impulse determines behavior is indeed true of animals. For example, as we previously noted, an animal is driven by hunger to look for food, and cannot resist doing so. Suppose, however, that a hungry jackal that is foraging for food spies a carcass, and has an intense desire to satisfy its hunger by eating it. Unfortunately for the jackal, a huge, ferocious tiger happens to be feasting on the carcass. The hungry jackal will not go anywhere near the carcass, not because it respects the property rights of the tiger, but because it does not want to get killed, which would surely happen if it tried to invade the tiger's territory. The drive to satisfy its hunger is opposed and overcome by the drive for survival, and so the jackal forgoes eating in order to escape the punishment of being killed by the tiger. In other words, *animals will resist an impulse if gratifying it is fraught with the possibility of retribution.*

Let us suppose that a person who is extremely money hungry is employed in a firm which turns over many millions of dollars each day. Being very savvy on computers, he has figured out a way to divert money from various accounts to his own, and could become very wealthy in a short period of time. His insatiable greed makes him consider this dishonest behavior. He realizes, however, that the auditors will undoubtedly have on their team a person who is equally computer-savvy, and there is a possibility that these transactions could be traced to him. If that were to occur, his ill-begotten money would be confiscated, he would be hit with a hefty fine of $50,000 or more, and would be sentenced to a long prison term for computer crime. Because the possible consequences of gratifying his greed are too formidable, he does not risk doing so, and abstains from committing the crime. In this case the philosophers are correct. The greedy impulse conflicted with the fear of retribution, and since the latter was the stronger of the two, he desisted from the act. His decision not to steal was not a moral decision, but was very much like the jackal's decision to forego trying to satisfy its hunger because of the fear of being killled by the tiger. This decision was therefore not a uniquely human decision.

When does a person become uniquely human? *When he resists a bodily impulse in the absence of the possibility of any form of retribution, solely because he considers it to be morally wrong.* This is something which no animal can accomplish.

Suppose a man from a town in northern Maine attends a business convention in Hawaii. There is not a single soul there who knows him. He is seized by a temptation to do something immoral, and he knows that there is no possibility that he will be discovered. Furthermore, given the current libertarian attitudes in society, even the exposure of an immoral act may have little consequence. However, he resists yielding to temptation because he believes such behavior to be morally wrong. He denies a strong physical impulse *in absence of any threat of punishment,* solely on a moral-ethical basis. This is where man rises above the animal level. No animal can make a moral-ethical decision. Man is thus the only living creature that has *true freedom of choice,* and the capacity to be *truly free* is therefore uniquely human, and is a cornerstone of spirituality.

In my work treating addicts, I point out to them that addiction is the most absolute type of slavery the world has ever known. A person who has become addicted to drugs is likely to do things he had never thought possible, but when he is in the grip of addiction, the drug is a ruthless, totalitarian dictator, and he will do whatever is necessary to obtain his drug. The addict completely loses the unique human distinction of being *free*.

Addiction to drugs is not the only way a person may lose his freedom. We are often dominated by other drives, which we may not recognize as tyrannical. Yet, when we are under their dominance, we have lost our precious freedom of choice, much the same as the drug addict.

There are people who are true *workaholics*, and cannot tear themselves away from the office, even though they know they should be with the family. There are people who are so ego driven to achieve recognition or acclaim that they will do anything to get it. There are people who have an insatiable desire to have more money, and cannot restrain themselves from trying to further increase their already enormous wealth, even though they could not possibly consume what they have in a thousand lifetimes. And of course, there are people who very much want to live and be healthy, but cannot resist the impulse to smoke cigarettes, even though they are fully aware of the toxic and even lethal effects of smoking. There are people who, try as they might, succumb to the urge to eat far more than is healthy. In all these situations, something has wrested the freedom of choice from the person. Whenever this happens, the person has become a slave to his particular habit.

In the Haggadah *From Bondage to Freedom* (*Mesorah Publications,* 1995), I pointed out that the emphasis given to the Exodus from Egypt indicates that Passover is not merely an "independence day" celebration which lasts a full week. In addition to a full week of total abstinence from *chametz,* which follows several weeks of meticulous housecleaning and virtual sterilization of the kitchen, we also declare that each Shabbos and all the festivals commemorate the Exodus. The Torah associates many mitzvos with the Exodus: *tefillin, tzitzis, kashrus,* redemption of the firstborn, forbidden relationships, to name just a few. In fact, the basis of our very belief in G–d is related to the Exodus, as is evident in the first commandment: "I am the Lord, your G–d, Who has delivered you from the land of Egypt."

The repeated reference to the Exodus is to remind us that we are not to be enslaved, neither by a despot such as Pharaoh nor by any habit which becomes despotic and deprives us of our free will. If we feel we cannot throw off the shackles of a habit, we are reminded that G–d delivered us from the enslavement of Egypt, and that if we make a sincere attempt at overcoming our tyrannical habit and turn our lives and will over to G–d as is stated in *Ethics of the Fathers* (2:4), He will deliver us from our despotic habit as well. Just as in the Exodus the deliverance did not occur until the enslavement surpassed our tolerance and we cried out to G–d (*Exodus* 2:23), so with any habit that has taken over control of our lives and has enslaved us, we must feel this enslavement as intolerable, because only then will we make a sincere effort to break loose from its grip and invoke G–d's help in becoming free.

Western civilization extols freedom as an inalienable human right. Unfortunately, this love of liberty is too often restricted to political freedom, but in our daily lives we may be oblivious to the fact that we have surrendered our freedom to various drives, and are not masters over our behavior any more than are brute beasts.

Nothing is more central to Jewish spirituality than free will. In his last words to us, Moses said, "I have set before you life and death, blessing and curse, *and you should choose life* ... to love G–d and to hearken to His words" (*Deuteronomy* 30:19-20). Moses was not referring to physical life, because we see many people who are physically alive although they do not observe the word of G–d. Moses was referring to spiritual life, to live at a human level rather than at an animal level, which constitutes the death of the human spirit. Spiritual life is *choice*, and we have freedom of choice only when we break loose from the tyranny of our physical, animalistic drives. The Talmud says, "Freedom is inscribed on the Tablets (of the Ten Commandments)" (*Ethics of the Fathers* 6:2).

As we have noted, animals are dominated by their bodily drives and do not have free choice. Angels, while totally spiritual, are agents of G–d to carry out assigned missions, and they do not have a choice to obey or disobey. Of all creations, man is the only one that has choice, and in this way man is likened to G–d, because only G–d and man are free to act. Rabbi Dessler says that this is precisely what is meant by man being created in the "image of G–d"; i.e., that man is like G–d in not being compelled in his actions. How careful we must be in using the faculty that we alone share with G–d!

Our pride and dignity should cause us to rebel against anything that deprives us of our uniquely human trait, that of freedom of choice. When we achieve true freedom, we advance our spirituality.

34

Homo Sapiens After All?

At the outset, we were very critical of the scientific description of man as *Homo sapiens*, because it is evident that man has many other features in addition to intellect. Perhaps we were a bit too harsh, because if we translate *sapiens* as "wisdom" rather than "intellect," we may have not only an acceptable but also an accurate description of man. As the Talmud says, "If you have wisdom, you lack nothing; if you lack wisdom, you have nothing" (*Vayikra Rabbah* 1:6). However, this assumes that we will be wise enough to avoid allowing our judgment to be influenced by our physical drives.

The Talmud states that had the Torah not been given to us, we would have been expected to learn some types of proper behavior by observing other creatures. Thus, we would have been expected to learn respect of property rights by observing ants, modesty from observing cats, fidelity from observing doves, etc. (*Eruvin* 100b). However, without Torah to guide us, is it not possible that we would have learned plundering from tigers and promiscuity from dogs? What would have directed us to learn only the salutary traits?

The answer is that we would have been expected to exercise our intellect, and to realize that our very nature militates against indulging in self-gratifying behavior.

The Steipler Gaon points out that if we were to see a child wearing a jacket whose sleeves extend far beyond his hands, his trouser legs dragging behind him, and his hat covering his nose, we would immediately conclude that the child put on his father's clothes. Obviously, clothes of these proportions were not intended for a child. Similarly, if gratifying our impulses was the purpose of our existence, why would we have been given so marvelous an intellect? Are not animals far more content than intelligent humans? Are not the wise words of Solomon self-evident: "Whosoever increases wisdom, increases worry"? (*Ecclesiastes* 1:18). Animals do not have anxiety or panic attacks. They do not worry about being able to afford education for their children, or how they will be able to marry them off. They do not think ahead as to how they will be cared for in their old age. They are not concerned whether the tampering with the ozone layer will jeopardize life on earth. Just think of the kinds of things man worries about and agonizes over, and you will come to the conclusion that animals are far more content and much less distressed than humans. If the purpose of man on earth is to gratify his impulses, then the intellect with which he was endowed is counter-productive. Operating by instinct rather than by reasoning would have resulted in far less misery in the history of mankind. Man's being endowed with intelligence indicates that he was created for something other than being content.

Simple application of reason, if not distorted by desire, would lead us to the truth. This is how the patriarch Abraham came to the knowledge of G–d. He realized that paganism was nothing other than man creating his own gods and his own religion so that he could give sanction to fulfilling all his desires. Greek paganism went beyond that, ascribing to the gods themselves the basest behaviors of greed, envy, anger, and lust. It was Abraham's application of reason, unadulterated by desire and directed solely to the discovery of truth, that led him to the true G–d. Once we have belief in G–d as the Creator of the world, we are well on the way to spirituality. The Talmud states that Moses gave us 613 commandments, which David condensed into 11 principles, which Isaiah condensed into six, Michah into three, and Habakkuk into the single principle: "A righteous person lives with *emunah* (belief in G–d)" (*Makkos* 24a). If unadulterated and unbiased reasoning is applied, one can reason from belief in G–d to observance of all 613 mitzvos. This is why it was possible for Abraham to observe all the mitzvos long before they were given in the Torah (*Yoma* 28b).

Sechel (good sense) is the key to spirituality. Putting the *sechel* into operation will lead a person to a proper understanding of the purpose of life and how to fulfill it. The chassidic work, *Tanya*, by Rabbi Shneur Zalman, elaborates on how one can proceed from intellect to emotions, and teaches that, indeed, proper application of intellect can give rise to proper emotions. However, the slightest deviation from the sincere search for truth can lead the reasoning process to totally erroneous goals. It is much like a missile that is directed at the moon, where a deviation of no more than the most infinitesimal fraction of an inch at the point of origin can cause it to miss the target by many miles. If a person remains on a true course, reasoning can lead him to proper traits and behavior.

The problem, of course, is that man is exceedingly vulnerable to being misled in his judgments, as evidenced by Adam and Eve, whose desire for the forbidden fruit led them to justify eating it in defiance of G–d's command to the contrary. It is therefore necessary for us to be given explicit instructions by the Torah, since our judgment is unreliable.

Now that we have the Torah as our guide, we should apply our reasoning powers to know how to live a proper and righteous life. Exercising this capacity within the framework of Torah will make us spiritual.

35

The World as a Tool

ou might point out a glaring omission in the distinguishing features between man and animals, one which every schoolchild seems to know — that man is the only creature that uses tools; hence the use of tools should be a spiritual trait. This might strike us as a bit odd. What does the use of tools have to do with spirituality?

The omission of this feature in our definition of spirituality was not a dereliction, but very much intended. Contrary to what people may think, some animals *do* use tools. Chimpanzees have been observed to use sticks to dig for something they wanted, and some animals who eat crustaceans have been observed to throw the shell against a rock to crush it. These may be primitive uses of tools, but nevertheless the category of use of tools is not exclusively human.

There is one application of tool-use that is very exclusive, and that is *to perceive the entire world as a tool.* When people speak of means and ends, they generally refer to both as being within this world, the ends as well as the means. Judaism teaches otherwise, and this is very clearly stated by RaMCHaL in *Path of the Just.* Man was not created for this world, says RaMCHaL. Inasmuch as a benevolent being wishes to bestow good and kindness, G–d, Who is the ultimate good, created man in order that He should be able to reward him. However, reward that is not earned cannot be fully enjoyed and appreciated, and the recipient of unearned reward may feel humiliated, similar to someone who receives alms. Therefore, G–d put man in this world where he is faced with many challenges, and by overcoming those challenges man earns his reward. The challenges are in the form of the many temptations to which a person is subject, and when a person overcomes these challenges by following the will of G–d, he then earns the reward. This world is but a "tool," an instrument whereby a person can fashion and "build" his home in the World to Come.

The Talmud frequently states this principle. "This world is like a corridor before the World to Come. Prepare yourself in the corridor so that you may enter the banquet hall" (*Ethics of the Fathers* 4:22). And again, "One who prepares his meals on Friday will have what to eat on Shabbos, but if one does not prepare on Friday, he will have nothing for Shabbos" (*Avodah Zarah* 3a). The "banquet hall" and "Shabbos" are the World to Come, and we can participate in the great "banquet" on the great "Shabbos" only if we prepare ourselves for them, and that is why we are in this world — to prepare for the World to Come. This world is only a tool to be utilized in our quest.

The Midrash states that the patriarch Jacob, after having suffered from the hostility of Esau and the deceit of Laban, finally returned to his paternal homeland, and hoped that he could now find peace in his old age. "You want tranquility in this world?" G–d said. "That cannot be. Tranquility is reserved for the World to Come" (*Rashi, Genesis* 37:2). This world is one of travail. We were put here to struggle, and while we should judiciously partake of the goods in this world, our primary function here is not earthly pleasure, but preparation for the incomparable pleasure of being in the immanent presence of the glory of G–d in the Eternal World.

The futility of earthly pleasures is the theme of *Ecclesiastes*, and the foolish attitude that some people may have that their earthly lives and belongings are eternal is summarized in psalm 49, which is appropriately read in the home of a mourner. Too often it is only the reality of death that makes us come to terms with our mortality, and it is then that we may at least momentarily understand our presence in this world as being nothing more than a sojourn. David summarizes this in the last verse of that psalm: "Man is glorious, but does not understand. He is likened to the silenced animals" (*Psalms* 49:21). Indeed, a person who is deluded into thinking that this world is all there is may justly be compared to an animal. It is tragic that with all man's intellect, which is his pride and glory, he may not have a concept of life surpassing that of an animal.

The following story has been variously ascribed to a number of *tzaddikim*.

A wealthy man visited the tzaddik, and was shocked to see the tzaddik's meager dwelling place, where one room served as his dining room, kitchen, bedroom, and living room. He remarked to the tzaddik that he does not understand how a person can live in such austere space.

"And how do you live?" the tzaddik asked.

"I have a spacious home, with a bedroom, living room, dining room, kitchen. and study."

"And when you travel on the road for business, do you also have such spacious living quarters?" the tzaddik asked.

"No," the man answered. "When I am on the road I have a single room in a hotel."

"It is the same with me," the tzaddik said. "In my eternal home I hope to have very comfortable accommodations. But on this earth, I am just a traveler doing my business, and like you, one room is enough for me when I am on the road."

Many people are displeased with their lot in this world, and their discontent may consume them. If we see this world as only a tool by which we earn our eternal life, we may rid ourselves of this discontent.

A truly spiritual person has a proper perspective of this world as a tool, and is consequently much more contented than those who believe their earthly existence to be all they have.

36

Insatiability

Our observation of animals reveals that animals have physiologic limits and do not indulge beyond that. To the best of my knowledge, tigers and deer and foxes do not have obesity problems. Animals that have been domesticated may take on human habits and become obese, but in their natural habitat animals remain within their physiologic limits of food intake. This is also true of their other bodily drives as well.

Human beings are much different. Many people eat far more than their nutritional need, and may sleep to excess, work to excess, hoard money to excess, and seek acclaim to excess. In contrast to animals, humans have turned the physiologic drive of lust into a major industry, with indulgence being dangerous as well as immoral. Why are people not guided by built-in physiologic controls like animals? Is it conceivable that G–d would have given animals greater perfection than His crowning jewel of creation?

The answer is that man does have internal physiologic controls which are every bit as efficient as those of animals. However, whereas an animal is comprised of nothing other than physiology, man has an additional component, which is the *spirit*. Because the goal of the spirit is a relationship with infinite G–d, this component does not have any limits. Inasmuch as G–d is infinite in every way, the drive to identify with G–d can never be fully satisfied. The closer the relationship of a person to G–d, the greater is his awareness of the *Ein Sof* (Infinite One), and the greater is the feeling of being distant from identifying with Him. Thus, in contrast to animals, man has a drive which is indeed insatiable and cannot be otherwise.

However, man is subject to the influence of the *yetzer hara*, which has the ability to distort a person's judgment and perception. When any human drive is frustrated, there is a consequent displeasure which one seeks to relieve. Our experience tells us that food relieves the displeasure of hunger, water relieves the displeasure of thirst, sleep relieves the displeasure of exhaustion, etc. When a person lacks spiritual fulfillment, he has a feeling of discontent similar to that of not having provided the hunger and thirst drives with what they crave. However, in the case of the spirit the *yetzer hara* steps in and prevents a person from recognizing the truth, which is that he is lacking in spirituality. Having been blinded to the truth, a person may attempt to relieve this displeasure by means of other things that have worked to relieve other displeasures, such as food, alcohol, drugs, money, acclaim, etc. These are as inappropriate for satisfying the cravings of the spirit as water is for exhaustion or as sleep is for hunger. Instead of recognizing the obvious, the person who is deluded by the *yetzer hara* continues to turn to inappropriate methods to satisfy what are actually his spiritual yearnings, and this may result in the indulgences to excess that we witness in humans.

Virtually all of a person's capacities can be directed to either favorable or unfavorable goals, and this is the principle of *bechirah* (free choice). Man has free choice in the area of ethical-moral behavior. In his last words to the Israelites, Moses cautioned them, "I have set before you life and the good (on the one hand) and death and the evil (on the other hand) … and you should choose life" (*Deuteronomy* 30:19). Why was this necessary? What fool would choose death? The answer is that we are vulnerable to the deluding wiles of the *yetzer hara* that can make us think that evil is good.

Man has the trait of craving infinity. If he chooses wisely, he directs this craving toward its proper goal: identification with G–d. If he allows himself to be deluded by the *yetzer hara,* he may misdirect this craving with the result being an endless pursuit of things which cannot satisfy the craving for spirituality. Some of these pursuits may actually take on an addictive quality, possibly even to the point of altering his physiology so that breaking away from the addiction becomes extremely difficult.

The Jewish ethical works often refer to the trait of *histapkus* (being satisfied with one's essential needs) as being a characteristic of spirituality. We can now understand why this is so. A spiritual person has identified his spiritual yearnings and seeks to satisfy them by those actions and behaviors which are appropriate for them, i.e., those which the Torah has indicated will bring him into a more intimate relationship with G–d. What remains then are the physiologic drives which are rather easily satisfied and for which there are internal controls. Hence our *tzaddikim* were able to be happy with very austere living quarters, simple clothing, and food which was just sufficient to provide for their nutritional needs.

We may think of our *tzaddikim* as having made great sacrifices by depriving themselves of worldly pleasures, which indeed would constitute greatness. However, their achievements were even greater, in that their pursuit of spirituality was such that their worldly needs and desires were minimal, and they did not feel this to be a sacrifice, hence they could be truly happy with an existence that others would consider as deprivation.

Our Torah personalities were well aware that pursuit of luxuries can be insatiable, and that just as a person addicted to alcohol may be catapulted into a dangerous binge with even a single drink, so might the appetite for luxuries be set in motion with the slightest bit of excess. They were therefore on alert against any lapse in their frugality.

In Jerusalem there lived a Torah scholar, Reb Pesach Truker, who was a follower of the Maggid of Villkomer. The two spent many hours of the day and night together in prayer and Torah study, and were inseparable friends. One day, Reb Pesach detected a change in the Maggid's demeanor, and the latter began quoting sources from Torah literature on the evils of indulgence in excesses, and how this could result in severe spiritual ruin. Reb Pesach, who lived a most frugal life, could not understand why he was being reprimanded for indulging, and finally asked the Maggid why he was repeatedly focusing on the evils of indulging.

"Several weeks ago," the Maggid said, "when I was at your home, I noticed a silk tablecloth on your table. That is how it begins, Reb Pesach. You may think this is harmless, but I tell you that this may pick up momentum and result in disaster."

Reb Pesach responded, "Let me tell you the history of that tablecloth. Many years ago, as a young man in Kovno, one of its wealthy citizens, Reb Eliezer Freidin, fell sick. I visited him regularly, and learned Torah with him during his illness. When he recovered, he wanted to compensate me for my time and effort, but I told him that I would not accept any payment for doing a mitzvah.

"About a month ago, I received a package from Kovno, accompanied by a letter from Reb Eliezer's children. The letter stated that he had *died and had specified in his will that they send me this tablecloth, and that he would consider it a privilege to have it used in Jerusalem.*

"My wife suggested I return it, and this was my first impulse as well. However, I reflected that this might be an insult to the family. Furthermore, it is a mitzvah to fulfill the wishes of the departed, so I decided to keep it."

The Maggid nodded his assent, then said, "I understand your position, Reb Pesach. However, it makes little difference how one acquires a luxury item. The tendency is to expand upon it, and this can carry you away." They then agreed to ask the opinion of Rabbi Shmuel Salant, who was then the Rabbi of Jerusalem.

After due consideration, Rabbi Shmuel said, "It is true that we should fulfill the last wishes of Reb Eliezer that his tablecloth be used in Jerusalem. However, it is also true that yielding to any luxury may create a craving for more. Let us therefore do this. Cover your table with this silk cloth, but put a plain cloth over it so that it remains concealed."

Many would consider this to be much ado about nothing. However, our Torah scholars were aware of human nature, and knew that even a spiritual person might fall victim to the desire for the "better things in life."

The endless pursuit of worldly desires is fraught with frustration, and Solomon stated this quite clearly, "The wealth of the rich person does not allow him to sleep" (*Ecclesiastes* 5:11). Much like the drug addict who is driven to use more and more drugs to satisfy his insatiable craving, the person who pursues riches has no peace regardless of how much wealth he amasses. The constant pursuit of spirituality, however, even though it, too, is endless, is not at all frustrating, because in contrast to physiologic drives which have limits, it is the nature of the drive for spirituality to be limitless, and the fulfillment and gratification of the spiritual drive is the *process* rather than the goal. This was stated by the Rabbi of Kotzk who commented on the verse, "You shall seek G–d and you shall find Him" (*Deuteronomy* 4:29), as meaning the seeking *is* the finding, which means that for spirituality the goal *is* the process. It has therefore been aptly said that we are not judged according to where we are on the ladder of spirituality, but according to whether we are ascending or descending.

Just a bit of clear thinking should enable us to realize that this world is but a tool whereby we can achieve spirituality, and we can come to this realization if we do not allow our thinking to be muddled by the *yetzer hara*. Solomon summarized this in just a few words wherein he pointed out the futility of worldly pursuits. "G–d made man straight, but they (mankind) sought too many calculations" (*Ecclesiastes* 7:29). We were created with the ability to follow a simple, straight path, but we may fail to reach our spiritual goal if we complicate things and deviate onto many side roads that lead to nowhere except frustration.

37

Spirituality Within the Family

I n recent years there has been an unprecedented incidence of disruption of families. Certainly there were cases in the past of marriages being dissolved, of children deviating from parental values, of young people breaking away from their families, and of abusive relationships within the family. However, there is little doubt that the prevalence of these unfortunate occurrences has increased significantly. There are probably a number of factors that have contributed to this sorry state, but high on the list is lack of *spirituality*.

We have all attended many weddings, and have listened as the Rabbi chanted the *sheva berachos* (seven blessings) of the marriage ritual. The first of these is, "Blessed is G–d Who created everything for His glory." Although we heard this many times, how often have we given any thought as to the relevance of this *berachah* to marriage? The *berachos* which refer to the joy and happiness of the bride and groom come toward the end of the ceremony, but the first statement the young couple hears after the giving of the ring has joined them as husband and wife is that G–d created the entire world solely for His glory. This is certainly a fine thought, but seems to be no more relevant to marriage than to eating matzah on Passover or blowing the *shofar* on Rosh Hashanah. Why did our sages include it in the marriage ritual, and why is it given priority over other *berachos* that seem to be more appropriate?

It is clear that our sages wished to convey an all-important message to the couple. For a marriage to be successful and happy, and for the future family to be wholesome, the marriage must be based on and dedicated to the concept that *everything in the world must be directed toward the greater glory of G–d.* If a marriage is not founded on this principle, it is on very uncertain ground.

Few marriages in Western civilization are based on this principle. The overwhelming majority are based on mutual attraction, whether physical or otherwise. The young man "loves" this young woman because he feels that she can satisfy his needs, and vice versa.

The word "love" must be understood.

T*he Rabbi of Kotzk once met a young man who was clearly enjoying a fish delicacy.*

"Why are you eating fish?" the Rabbi asked.

The young man appeared puzzled. "Why? Because I love fish."

"Oh, you do, do you?" the Rabbi said. "And because you love the fish so much that is why you took it out of the water where it was thriving, killed it, and cooked it. You do not love the fish, young man. It is yourself that you love, and because the fish tastes pleasant to you, you killed it and ate it."

The Rabbi's point is both obvious and profound. We may refer to "loving" someone else because that person pleases us, but in that case it is really ourselves that we love. A marriage that is based on this kind of love, "fish love" as it were, is on a shaky foundation. Inasmuch as the unspoken but nevertheless underlying condition of the contract is the satisfaction that the other person will provide, it is understandable that if either partner believes that some other person can better fulfill one's needs, the deal is off.

It is totally different if the marriage is based on an awareness that we are to dedicate our lives to the greater glory of G–d. If this is the *primary* goal and purpose of the marriage, then the mutual affection and the fulfillment of one's emotional needs, while certainly important, do not have to bear the survival of the relationship alone. While moments of friction or frustration may occur, they do not threaten the integrity of the relationship, because it is supported by the strength of mutual dedication to a higher goal.

The Talmud states it succinctly, "If man and woman merit, the presence of G–d is with them" (*Sotah* 17a).

This extends to the children as well. "There are three partners in a person: G–d, one's father, and one's mother" (*Kiddushin* 30b). Just as the strong bond between husband and wife results from the presence of G–d, so it is with parents and children.

It is germane here to relate a dialogue between Rabbi Bunim of Peshis'cha and a young student, Mendel, who subsequently became the Rabbi of Kotzk. "Young man," Rabbi Bunim asked, "where can G–d be found?"

The young Mendel replied by quoting the words of the prophet, "The entire universe is full of the glory of G–d" (Isaiah 6:3).

"Young man," the Rabbi said, "where can G–d be found?"

Mendel quoted the words of the Zohar, "There is no place that is devoid of Him."

The Rabbi persisted, "Young man, I am asking you, where can G–d be found?"

Mendel said, "If my answers do not satisfy you, then you tell me."

"G–d can be found," the Rabbi said, "wherever he is invited."

Yes, G–d is indeed everywhere, but His effective presence is only where He is welcomed. For example, the Talmud states that G–d shuns someone who is vain and arrogant (*Arachin* 15b). On the other hand, wherever there is observance of the Divine attributes, there

G–d's presence is prominent, because it is by emulating G–d's attributes that we bond with Him (*Shabbos* 133b), and essentially bring His presence to us.

If the motivation of a man and a woman approaching marriage would be *centrifugal,* the relationship would be of greater durability. In Judaism, the purpose of marriage is to raise a family and to transmit Torah teachings to the children. While mutual affection is certainly of great importance, it is not the sole quality upon which the marriage hinges.

Hence, even when differences arise that may threaten mutual affection, or if either partner thinks that his/her needs may be better served by someone else, the marriage is not seriously threatened. The overriding purpose of the marriage may maintain the bond, and may enable it to withstand any stresses and permit the wholesomeness of the relationship to be restored and even strengthened.

Centrifugal motivation is manifested by respect, and mutual respect is a pillar of the Jewish marriage. *Halachah* requires that the wife respect the husband, and with regard to the husband's attitude toward the wife, Rambam says, "He must respect her even more than he respects himself, and love her as he loves himself" (*Ishus* 19:15).

The Talmud relates that Rav Chiya's wife aggravated him to no end, yet he was most respectful toward her. Even though she caused him much distress, he respected her for her dedication in raising the children (*Yevamos* 63a). In modern times, such a marriage would likely have been terminated because of personal dissatisfaction.

In a world which champions "doing one's thing," marriages are often based on optimizing one's own glory. The first message given to the newlyweds is that G–d created the world for His glory, hence their marriage should be dedicated to the glory of G–d rather than to their own.

In regard to parental respect, the Talmud (*Kiddushin* 30b) notes that the Torah finds a parallel between honoring one's father and mother, and honoring G–d. Parents who truly incorporate the *middos* of spirituality in their own lives in their relationship with one another and who have dedicated their marriage and the establishment of the family to the first of the seven *berachos*, to the greater glory of G–d rather than to their personal gratification, will likely imbue the household with the presence of G–d so that the children will honor both G–d and them.

Centrifugal motivation is equally important in the parent-child relationship. We all desire to have *nachas* (pleasure) from our children, but we must also remember that the parental responsibility is to provide their children with the training that will enable *them* to achieve the most in life. Where the child's goals and the parents' goals for them are congruent, there is no problem. However, if the two diverge, it is important to carefully analyze them, so that the parent does not impose something on the child which is not to the latter's advantage.

The *teshuvah* movement has resulted in children of parents who were not Torah observant taking on observance of mitzvos. The child may not be able to eat in the parents' non-kosher home, and may not be able to participate in family activities on Shabbos. Some parents may take offense at this because they interpret it as a rejection of their values and a personal insult to them, rather than considering what would be best for the child's well-being. Many parents are respectful of the child's new lifestyle, and are pleased that their child has adopted a system of values that is far above those of their hedonistic environment.

I visited a family which was non-observant, but who had made a very smooth adjustment to their son's adopting a strict Torah lifestyle. I marveled at the ease with which this had been accomplished, and was surprised that the loving relationship between this son and all other family members had not been affected in the least. The father, who is an internationally well-known figure, happened to mention to me that he had just canceled an important lecture tour to several major cities around the world because a younger son who was soon to graduate high school still had two more football games left in the season, and he wanted to be in the stands when his child played. It became clear to me why the adaptation to the older son's assuming a Torah lifestyle had been so smooth. A father who could cancel an international tour because he knew that his son wished him to cheer for him at the game was a father who had the older son's best interest at heart rather than his own, and this enabled him to see that the older son's new lifestyle was to his child's advantage, hence he did not consider it to be a rejection of the parents' values.

It should be readily apparent that spiritual people who

are centrifugally motivated, control their anger, are truthful, do acts of *chesed,* share in others' difficulties, sincerely rejoice in others' success, accept adversity with trust and faith in G–d, and develop all the other *middos* that comprise spirituality, are likely to have a household that has a minimum of conflict and friction among its members. We must remember that while the observance of the various mitzvos is all-important, it is the *middos* that create the atmosphere in the home. Many of our ethicists have stated that it is much easier to observe mitzvos than to develop *middos,* and that if we wish our homes to be wholesome, we must give great attention to developing the *middos* that comprise spirituality.

It is tragic that far too many families are affected by spouse abuse, child abuse, and/or elder abuse. All these abuses are an outgrowth of a preoccupation with one's own comfort, since the abuser feels that the victim is encroaching upon it. Families that are primarily dedicated to the greater glory of G–d are likely to be spared this modern day devastation.

The act of the giving of the ring in the marriage ceremony is referred to as *kiddushin,* or sanctification. The young couple is then told that their marriage can be permeated with holiness only if they will bear in mind that they, their marriage, and their children are all to be dedicated to the greater glory of G–d. The marriage ceremony is then completed with *nisuin,* which means elevation. When personal interests occupy a secondary position, the quality and viability of the marriage is greatly enhanced. A marriage based on spirituality is likely to be both happy and permanent.

38

Protecting Our Spirituality

e have defined the "spirit" as being the aggregate of all the traits that are unique to man and that distinguish him from animals. The spirit essentially constitutes the identity of man, because without it he is little more than a biped animal that has a more extensive vocabulary than other animals. We can now better understand the Talmudic statement that "the wicked are considered dead even during their lifetime" (*Berachos* 18b). This is because in absence of spirituality, they lack the distinctly human component, and although they breathe and move about, it is the animal part of them that lives; but as true humans, i.e., people with a spirit, they are indeed dead.

The instinct for self-survival is very powerful in both man and animal, and causes us to take steps to protect our lives. We instinctively avoid danger, and we try to care for ourselves to avoid injury to our bodies, except perhaps for those people whose denial of reality allows them to continue smoking. It would seem that inasmuch as our lives as true human beings are dependent on our implementation of the components of the spirit, because without the spirit we are "dead" as humans, we would take equal precautions to protect our spirit from injury. Why is it that we so often fail to protect our spirit, and indeed, we sometimes consciously jeopardize it, as for example, when we expose ourselves to the noxious influence of immoral material in the media? One would think that there would be a "self-survival" instinct to protect the spirit similar to that which protects the animal body.

The prophet Isaiah addressed this issue and answered the question in his statement, "The heart of this nation has grown fat, its ears are heavy (clogged), and its eyes are pasted shut, lest it see with its eyes, hear with its ears, and understand with its heart, for then they would repent and be healed" (*Isaiah* 6:10). These powerful words contain a psychological truth, and indeed, our example of the person who jeopardizes his health by smoking cigarettes is appropriate.

The pursuit of comfort and the avoidance of discomfort can be so powerful that they set up a *denial*, whereby the person is unable to perceive reality. An intelligent person who otherwise cares for his health may continue to smoke because *he does not believe that he will be harmed.* Health care professionals who observe the suffering of patients with cancer or emphysema may be observed to be standing in front of the hospital smoking cigarettes. How can this be? Because the pleasure they get from smoking and the discomfort of discontinuing to smoke set up a denial which blinds them to the obvious. As Isaiah said, if seeing, hearing, and understanding threaten to deprive us of pleasure, we may not see, hear, or understand even the obvious.

The Torah says, "You shall protect your souls" (*Deuteronomy* 4:15), and although this verse is cited as the scriptural dictate that we care for our physical health, the context of the verse indicates that it refers primarily to our spiritual well-being, for the Torah continues with a very stern warning against idolatry. We know idolatry to be nothing more than a way to sanction one's immoral behavior, as the Talmud states, "The Israelites never believed in idols. They simply wanted to gain social approval for immoral acts" (*Sanhedrin* 63b). The Torah therefore cautions us to protect our spirit because we are vulnerable to be seduced into denying it by the desire to gratify our physical urges.

In working with people addicted to alcohol, we find that they do not curtail their drinking until some serious crisis occurs to shake them loose from their denial. It is tragic that this is necessary, because in the case of smoking, the crisis may be a lung condition which is irreversible and often fatal. The denial of lack of spirituality is also not likely to be overcome unless some type of crisis occurs to bring a person to the realization that he has lost the essence of his humanity. Unfortunately, as with smoking, behavior that is devoid of spirituality may have grave and seemingly irreversible consequences. Ironically, it is precisely the awareness of the gravity of these consequences that may reinforce the denial. One may think, "What's the use of my trying to change? After all I have done, I cannot possibly become spiritual. I might as well just continue living the way I am." This thought may be either conscious or unconscious, but in either case, it may militate against coming to the awareness that one is lacking in spirituality.

Judaism teaches that there is never any reason to despair of becoming spiritual. Rabbi Akiva was not only illiterate at the age of 40, but also despised Torah scholars (*Pesachim* 49b), yet he became one of the greatest *tzaddikim* of Jewish history, who in some respects was considered superior even to Moses (*Menachos* 49b)! Rabbi Shimon ben Lakish, an outstanding sage of the Talmud, was the leader of a band of thieves before he turned to Torah. Throughout our history there were many instances of people who were anything but spiritual in their earlier years, but went on to become paragons of spirituality.

Torah literature is replete with the inordinate greatness a person can achieve with *teshuvah*. So much so that the Talmud states that a person who makes the turn to spirituality may have an advantage over someone who was spiritual from the start (*Berachos* 34b).

R abbi Levi Yitzchak of Berditchev met a man who was an avowed sinner. "How I envy you!" the Rabbi said.

"You envy me?" the man said. *"Surely you are mocking me."*

"No, not at all," the Rabbi said. *"The Talmud states that when a person does sincere teshuvah, all his sins will be converted into merits. One day you will do teshuvah, and you will have far more merits than I have."*

Within each of us there is a G–dly *neshamah,* a spark of spirituality which can never be extinguished. It may lie dormant for years, but just like the molten lava at the core of the earth which pushes its way to the surface through crevices, and when it breaks through the surface erupts with a tremendous force, so do the spark of the *neshamah* and the nucleus of dignity within us slowly push to the surface, and will one day break through to our awareness, and we will then realize that we dare not be less than we can be.

There is never any reason to despair of achieving great spirituality.

How High
Spirituality?

We have alluded to the fact that as is the case with animals, all man's biologic drives should have limits, and the reason people indulge in excesses is because man does have an infinite drive, which is to have an ever closer relationship with G–d. The *yetzer hara,* however, blinds a person to the true nature of his infinite drive, and when the person feels a discontent, the *yetzer hara* makes him think it is because he is lacking money, food, acclaim, amusement, luxuries, etc. Hence the person engages in a futile pursuit of contentment by indulgence, and can never be free of discontent because he is not satisfying the real infinite drive.

But just what *is* the level a human being can be expected to reach? What is the spiritual goal for which one must aim?

The Midrash answers this with its comment on the verse, "You shall be holy because I, your G–d, am holy" (*Vayikra* 19:2). The Midrash says, "When I tell you to be holy, you might think that you should be as holy as I am, therefore I tell you that My holiness is superior to yours" (*Vayikra Rabbah* 24:9). Rabbi Chaim Shmulevitz cites this Midrash and asks, "How could the Talmudic authors even contemplate that a human being might be expected to aim to be as holy as G–d Himself? That is a patent absurdity which hardly needs refutation!" Rabbi Shmulevitz answers that the authors of the Midrash had a far better concept of the infinite greatness of G–d than we do, and if they said that it was necessary for Scripture to point out that man cannot achieve the holiness of Almighty G–d, it is because if we really knew the potential greatness of man, we might well think that it *is* within man's capability to achieve the holiness of G–d. That is how we must understand the enormous potential for spirituality had by a human being.

The Talmud states that the sage, Shimon Amsoni, explained that wherever the Torah uses the word "*es*," which has no meaning of its own, it indicates that we must add something to the noun that follows; i.e., the word *es* makes the subsequent noun more inclusive. Shimon did so wherever the Torah used the word *es*, until he came to the verse which says that man must revere G–d, and here Scripture says *es Hashem*, which according to his thesis, would mean that there is someone else in addition to G–d that man must revere as much as one reveres G–d. Inasmuch as this is impossible, he concluded that his thesis must be in error, and that *es* does not indicate that the subsequent noun is more inclusive, because the Torah could not be telling us to revere anything or anyone as we revere G–d.

The Midrash goes on to say that when Rabbi Akiva came along, "he" interpreted even this *es* to be inclusive, and said that it means we must revere Torah scholars just as we revere G–d. We may ask: Why could Shimon Amsoni not have interpreted the verse the way Rabbi Akiva did?

One of the commentaries gives us a brilliant interpretation, but we must reread the Midrash carefully. The elusive *es* was not explained until Rabbi Akiva came along and "he" stated that the *es* refers to Torah scholars. What is the antecedent of "he"? We assume that it refers to Rabbi Akiva, who provided the interpretation.

Not so, says this commentary. The "he" refers to Shimon Amsoni. What happened was that Shimon was stymied by the question: How is it possible for the Torah to equate anyone or anything as deserving the reverence one should have for G–d? He was therefore unable to interpret this *es*. But then Rabbi Akiva came along, and when Shimon saw the overwhelming spiritual greatness of Rabbi Akiva, he understood why it was possible for the Torah to demand that we revere Torah scholars as we do G–d, and he realized that his thesis about the interpretation of *es* as inclusive was correct after all. If a human being can achieve the greatness of Rabbi Akiva, he indeed does deserve to share the reverence we have for G–d. This is an indication of the potential greatness which lies within man.

The Midrash (*Bereishis Rabbah* 8:9) also states that when Adam was created, the angels wished to worship him. Again, an indication that man can be so great that he can be mistaken for G–d!

Just as Shimon Amsoni was able to appreciate the enormous spirituality of Rabbi Akiva, so can we appreciate the spirituality of the Torah personalities who lived close to our time. And lest we think that the holiness of these Torah giants might equal that of G–d, Scripture indicates that G–d's holiness is superior to all.

The Chafetz Chaim, who dedicated his life to Torah and supported himself by a small store which his wife managed, lived just several decades ago. As soon as the store produced enough income to support them for that day, it was closed until the next day. His trust in G–d was like that of our ancestors in the desert, who trusted that G–d would provide their needs each day, and there was no reason to worry about tomorrow. Was he superhuman? No, just human in the full understanding of the term.

It was the Chafetz Chaim who was overheard saying at the funeral of his son, "Master of the Universe! I can no longer give my son the great love I had for him. I will now give that love to You." Is this superhuman? No, just truly human.

Just over 100 years ago lived the *tzaddik* of Sanz, whose compassion for the poor was such that he gave away everything he had to *tzedakah*. His *Kiddush* cup was pawned promptly after Shabbos and the money distributed to the poor. On Friday his *chassidim* would redeem the cup for him. If he was unable to fall asleep at night he searched the house to see whether there might be any money remaining that had not been given to *tzedakah,* because this was undoubtedly why he could not sleep. Was he superhuman? No, because he knew that the difference between humans and animals is that people are centrifugal and extend care to others. He was just being what he considered a human being.

Several generations earlier, Rabbi Levi Yitzchak of Berditchev complained of being hungry at the close of the Yom Kippur fast, but did not touch any of the food that was served. Instead, he took the volume *Succah* of the Talmud, to study the laws for the great festival of Succos that would begin in four days. Was he superhuman? No, not at all. It was just that the hunger of his spirit for Torah and mitzvos exceeded his body's hunger for food.

An eyewitness related that during the Holocaust, when Jews were shipped to the death camps in crowded cattle cars, they had gone for two days without water, and the weaker among them perished. Finally some water was brought aboard and small amounts were rationed to all those who had survived. When the Rabbi of Klausenburg received his ration, he did not drink it, but performed the ritual washing of the hands after sleep. Was he superhuman? We may think so, but many of us knew this great *tzaddik* to be mortal, but a truly spiritual human being whose thirst to fulfill a Rabbinic ordinance was greater than his thirst for water.

You will recall that earlier we noted that *forgiveness* was a spiritual trait. But just how far should we carry forgiveness?

Just a week before Rosh Hashanah, Rabbi Yosef Chaim Sonnenfeld presided over a beis din (rabbinical tribunal) which issued a verdict in a dispute between two litigants. One of the litigants felt that he had been wronged and that the decision of the tribunal was unjust. He and his family came to the Rabbi's home and vilified him with a most chutzpadik (audacious) diatribe, screaming insults at him. Rabbi Sonnenfeld sat quietly through the episode, but the Rabbi's wife broke out in tears.

At one point Rabbi Sonnenfeld arose and signaled them into silence. "If you are correct in your criticism of me, and the beis din was in error," he said, "then you have registered your complaint with G–d, Who will be my judge. I rendered my decision to the best of my ability, which is all I could do. If I was wrong, I pray that G–d will forgive me.

"However, if we were right ...," here the Rabbi raised his voice and spoke in a loud, firm tone, "if we were right in our judgment ...," the Rabbi paused a moment, and the aggressors turned pale with fear, expecting the Rabbi to pronounce a malediction and bring down the wrath of G–d upon them, "if we were right and you are wrong, then I wholeheartedly forgive you for your disre-spect and the agony you have caused me and my wife, and I sincerely wish that you be in-scribed in the Book of Life for a healthy and happy year."

A Rabbi who lived next door overheard the en-tire incident and said to Rabbi Sonnenfeld, "Granted, you chose to forgive them, because that is what tzaddikim do. But why did you do so promptly? It would have been better had you let them stew in their guilt and remorse, and then forgive them when they come to ask it of you."

Rabbi Sonnenfeld replied, "You must under-stand human nature. It is quite possible that when they would begin to realize they were wrong, they might rationalize their behavior and convince themselves that they were right after all. Instead of recognizing their mistake, they might try to defend it. If they came to believe they were right, they would not come to ask for forgiveness, and would enter Rosh Hashanah and Yom Kippur with the sin of defying a beis din. I would then be the cause of their receiving a harsh judgment from G–d."

"Now that I forgave them," the Rabbi contin-ued, "it is likely that when they rethink their behavior, the guilt will not be so intense as to lead to rationalization, and they will be truly re-morseful. They will then pray to G–d and receive His forgiveness. That is why I had to forgive them promptly."

Superhuman? No, just human, but in the full sense of the word.

And as for gratitude ...

R abbi Sholom Eisen had studied in the yeshiv- ah of Rabbi Issar Zalman Melzer, and when his son was to be bar mitzvah, he felt it only proper to invite the Rosh Yeshivah to the Kiddush in celebration of the occasion, never thinking that the sage would walk all the way to his home on Shabbos. How astonished all the guests were when, in the midst of the Kiddush, Rabbi Issar Zalman appeared, having climbed the four stories to R' Eisen's apartment! They expressed their wonder that the sage had so exerted him- self.

Rabbi Issar Zalman admitted, "Yes, it was a bit strenuous, but I felt indebted to Rabbi Sholom for a great kindness he did with me.

"After Reb Sholom invited me to his son's bar mitzvah, it suddenly occurred to me, 'Bar mitz- vah? Why, it seems as though I was just at Reb Sholom's wedding!' I realized how quickly the years had passed, and what do I have to show for them? This stimulated me to do teshuvah while I still have the opportunity to do so. I feel a debt of gratitude to Reb Sholom for bringing this about, and I had to come here as an expression of my appreciation."

This anecdote not only teaches us something about gratitude, but should also make us think — if the great *tzaddik*, Rabbi Issar Zalman, felt he must do *teshuvah*, what are we to say about ourselves?

We have noted that a characteristic of spiritual acts is that they are centrifugal rather than centripetal, hence our *tzaddikim* were always sensitive to the needs of others. Heaven forbid that they do anything that might offend someone in any way. The Talmud states that Rabbi Yochanan ben Zakkai, one of the foremost Jewish leaders and scholars, never waited for anyone to greet him first, although he was certainly the one who deserved to be honored. Rather, he greeted everyone he met, Jew and non-Jew alike (*Berachos* 17a).

> R abbi Shlomo Zalman Auerbach was on a bus in Jerusalem, when a young, scantily clad woman boarded and sat next to him. Rabbi Auerbach gently reached for the button to signal the driver that he wished to get off, and excused himself to the woman, "Pardon me, but I have to get off here."
>
> He then waited for the next bus. Rabbi Auerbach explained, "It was not proper for me to sit next to this woman, but if I simply moved away, this might offend her. Just because she was lacking in modesty is no grounds for causing her any embarrassment" (*HaTorah HaMisameches*, page 289).

◠◠

> F or several decades, Rabbi Auerbach lectured regularly at his yeshivah. Prior to each lecture,

he read a few paragraphs of the classical mussar text, Shaarei Teshuvah, Gates of Repentance, by Rabbeinu Yonah. Why? Because he was concerned that during the lecture, a student might ask a foolish question, and he might have a knee-jerk reaction, such as, "That question is totally out of order," and he would thereby humiliate the student. He therefore read some mussar before each lecture, to reinforce his sensitivity to be respectful to everyone (ibid., page 94).

⌒⌒

At one wedding where he was to officiate, Rabbi Auerbach was dissatisfied with the qualifications of one of the two designated witnesses. However, to reject this person was unthinkable. He therefore said to him, "Would you please do me a great favor? I am constantly asked to officiate at wedding ceremonies, but I have never had the privilege of being designated as a witness. Would you please trade places with me? You officiate and let me be a witness" (ibid., page 227). The requirements of halachah were met, but not at the cost of compromising someone's dignity.

Yes, it was indeed necessary for the Torah to remind us that human beings cannot achieve the holiness of G–d, because seeing Rabbi Akiva and those who followed in his footsteps, we might have thought otherwise.

40
Motivation and Deterrents

What should motivate a person to be spiritual?

Let us note that virtually everything in nature strives for its fulfillment. In heavily shaded forests, it is fascinating to see how branches of trees grow toward the places where they can receive the light of the sun, even circumventing rocks and other obstacles. It is even more fascinating to observe salmon swimming against the current and leaping over cascading water to reach their spawning place. Just as other things in creation, both animate and inanimate, have a natural tendency to reach the goals for which they were created, man must also have an innate urge to develop the *tzelem Elokim,* the Divine image, in which he was created.

The Talmud states that man is so dear to G–d that He created him in His own image, which, as we just said, should result in a natural urge for spiritual perfection, to be as akin to G–d as possible. But in contrast to other creations which have only an innate drive, man was *told* that he was created in the Divine image (*Ethics of the Fathers* 3:18), and he therefore has an additional advantage of being able, volitionally and consciously, to apply himself to the perfection of the goal for which he was created.

A person should also have sufficient pride and dignity not to allow himself to be less than he can be; but assessments of what constitutes human dignity may vary. For example, one person who discovers a slight stain on his garment will promptly exchange it for something spotless, whereas another person may not be bothered if he is seen in clothes that are less than immaculate. Similarly, the more a person feels the dignity of bearing a Divine *neshamah,* the more cautious he will be to protect it from becoming blemished.

Prior to the giving of the Torah at Sinai, G–d said to the Israelites, "You shall be for me a holy people" (*Exodus* 15:6). This was meant to be the motivation for accepting the Torah. It was not enough to be a people of great intellect, but rather a spiritual people.

That Judaism considers spirituality to be not only the goal of a person but also the ultimate purpose of Creation is indicated by the Talmudic comment on the verse which marks the end of Creation, "and it was evening and it was morning, *the* sixth day" (*Genesis* 1:31), upon which the

Talmud comments that *the* sixth day refers to the sixth day of Sivan, the day on which the Torah was given. The entire Creation was focused on the giving of the Torah, and had the Torah been rejected, there would have been no reason for the world to exist and G–d would have returned the earth to nothingness.

I recall as a child, when my father disapproved of something I was doing, his reprimand was, "*Es past nisht* (that does not become you)." I was being told to refrain from a particular behavior because I was too good for it, and it was beneath my dignity. The awareness of one's dignity should motivate a person to be spiritual.

The *Alter* of Slabodka said that a person should never, even momentarily, lose sight of his having been created in the likeness of G–d. As such, man serves as a testimony to G–d, and his very essence should bespeak the similarity between him and G–d. In a word, that is spirituality.

Other creatures are unfettered in fulfilling the purpose of their creation. There is nothing that discourages the branches from striving for the sunlight, and there is nothing to restrain the salmon from following their instinct to swim upstream against the current. But no other creature was given the capacity to exercise *bechirah* (free choice). While man, too, has an inborn instinct to fulfill himself, this is opposed by the *yetzer hara,* a powerful force that tries to stifle such fulfillment. In contrast to other living things, man must struggle against this destructive force in order to become the spiritual being he was intended to be.

The *yetzer hara* uses many tactics to obstruct the drive for spirituality. Firstly, it exploits the bodily drives in order to distort a person's judgment, and just as a bribe not only distorts a judge's reasoning but also renders him oblivious to facts (*Deuteronomy* 16:19), so does the *yetzer hara* utilize temptation to blind a person so that he misperceives reality.

Secondly, the *yetzer hara* deludes a person into thinking that improper behavior can be compatible with his sense of dignity. It is as though a dignified person discovers a stain on his clothing, but because he is too lazy to change clothes, thinks, "Why should I bother? No one will notice this anyway." Just as this person thinks that his appearance will not be affected by the unsightly stain, so the *yetzer hara* may convince a person that improper behavior will not impugn his dignity.

You will recall Rabbi Shneur Zalman's explanation of the Talmudic statement that "a person does not sin unless he takes leave of his mind" (*Sotah* 3a). He states that every Jew has an instinctive craving for a closeness and relationship with G–d. He points out that during the Inquisition, some Jews who were not at all observant of Torah went to the stake and accepted death rather than deny their G–d. This was because they realized that denying G–d would rupture their relationship with Him. The reason they were not observant of Torah was because they were unaware that any transgression can interrupt this relationship. We often hear people declare, "I am a Jew at heart," because they have been misled by the *yetzer hara* to believe that one can maintain a closeness with G–d even without observance of Torah. Were these people put to the test of denying G–d, they might well surrender their lives rather than do so. It is the *yetzer hara's* duping them into thinking that they can preserve a close relationship with

G–d in absence of Torah observance that enables them to sin, and this is the delusion that the Talmud is referring to as sin occurring only when one has taken leave of one's mind.

The *yetzer hara* deludes a person by means of a number of psychological processes which are referred to as the "defense mechanisms" of the mind. Chief among these is *denial*, whereby a person simply denies one or more aspects of reality. Denial is different than lying, because lying is conscious; i.e., the person knows the truth, but intentionally distorts it. Denial is unconscious; i.e., the person does not even realize that what he is thinking or saying is untrue. Denial occurs when a person intensely wishes to believe or not to believe something.

Denial can occur to anyone. The Torah relates that the matriarch Sarah laughed in disbelief when she heard the angel say that she would bear a child. When Abraham reprimanded her for her lack of faith, "Sarah *denied*, and said 'I did not laugh' because she feared" (*Genesis* 18:15). Rabbi Yitzchak Meir of Gur said that Sarah did not lie, but she was rather in *denial*, because she was so G–d fearing that she could not believe that she had questioned the angel's words.

It is not at all uncommon to observe people being in denial. Some people who have a symptom that may be of cancerous origin do not go to the doctor because they are terribly frightened that he might diagnose cancer, and this thought is so terrifying to them that the mind defends against it by blocking the awareness of the symptom. A person who has a severe alcohol problem may be in denial of his drinking, because awareness of it might be humiliating, and/or because such awareness would mean that he must stop partaking of alcoholic beverages, which he does not wish to do. Inasmuch as a person cannot make a proper adjustment to reality unless he has a correct perception of reality, the "defense mechanism" of denial is generally detrimental.

Denial is often supported by rationalization. One recovering alcoholic said, "I never once took a drink unless I decided it was the right thing to do at the time." If a person has a strong desire for something which is wrong, he may concoct many reasons to justify it as being right. In *Path of the Just,* RaMCHaL warns against the dangers of rationalization, because it may not only result in a person doing wrong, but may also prevent him from subsequently realizing that what he did was wrong, and so he will not do *teshuvah.*

The Torah relates that there were two populations that were destroyed: the people of Sodom and the generation of the flood. The Midrash states that the corruption of Sodom consisted of their legalizing every abomination. The people were convinced that what they were doing was right because it was sanctioned by law. There was therefore no possibility that they would ever do *teshuvah,* because *teshuvah* presupposes that one recognizes a mistake. Our generation should be particularly alert to this, because our legislatures and courts have used the tactics of Sodom, legalizing what society wishes to do.

The Midrash also states that the generation of the flood sinned in a manner that had no redress by law, such as stealing items that were beneath the minimum that one could appeal to the court. This led them to believe that what they were doing was within the law, and there was therefore no possibility that they would ever change their ways. These two populations were beyond redemption, and that is why they were destroyed.

Another common defense mechanism is projection, whereby a person denies his own defects and failings by attributing the defect to another person. The Talmud gives an example of this: When a person refers to someone else by a derogatory term it is because he himself has the fault which he is assigning to the other person (*Kiddushin* 70a). The Baal Shem Tov extended this further, and said that the world is a mirror, and that what you see in others is a reflection of yourself. The Baal Shem Tov was very much aware of the psychological mechanism of denial, and said that because a person is likely to deny his own defects, G–d arranges it so that he sees them in others, since this observation is not obstructed by denial. One must know, therefore, that the faults one notices in others are really one's own. One time the Baal Shem Tov saw a person violating Shabbos, and he wept profusely in *teshuvah* because he was certain that had he not somehow done something improper on Shabbos, he would not have been exposed to seeing *chillul* (violation) of Shabbos.

Inasmuch as a truly spiritual person should be intent on correcting his character defects, he should be aware of the mechanism of projection. Upon noticing a character defect in others, he should do a careful soul searching to discover where he, too, has some aspect of this defect and correct it.

"Blaming" is essentially a derivative of projection. If we can blame others for something, that absolves us of the need for self-improvement. I see this regularly in my work with alcoholics. "The reason I drink is because I am put under intolerable stress by my: wife, husband, son, daughter, father, mother, or employer." What the alcoholic is really saying is, "I don't need to make any changes in myself. You go ahead and get the person who is putting this excess stress on me to change his/her ways, and I'll be fine." Blaming others is simply an excuse for not exerting the necessary effort to make changes in oneself. The *yetzer hara* is sly enough to try and convince a person that what is actually a transgression will make him more spiritual. This can be seen from its first attempt in which it unfortunately succeeded in getting man to sin. In seducing Eve to eat from the forbidden fruit, the serpent (*yetzer hara*) said that "the fruit has the ability to make you like G–d" (*Genesis* 3:5). Since the fruit appeared to be delicious, temptation and delusion combined to cause the first sin.

These are but a few of the ways whereby the *yetzer hara* may delude a person and prevent his spiritual development. The most effective way to avoid being deluded by the *yetzer hara* is to follow the Talmudic advice, "Acquire for yourself a friend" (*Ethics of the Fathers* 1:6), upon which Rabbi Elimelech of Lizhensk comments that a person should have a friend in whom he can confide, and at the end of the day should review with his friend all of his actions and even his thoughts of that day. Inasmuch as the friend can be objective, he can alert a person to any distortions to which he may have been subjected by the *yetzer hara*, and one can then make the necessary corrections in oneself.

Since the *yetzer hara* may masquerade as an advocate

of spirituality and try to present a sin as being a mitzvah, one should heed the advice of the Talmud and "Make for yourself a teacher" (ibid.). A *halachic* authority can clarify whether what one wishes to do is really a mitzvah, or a subterfuge of the *yetzer hara*.

In chassidic and *mussar* writings, the *yetzer hara* is often referred to as the *nefesh habeheimis* (animal soul), because by deterring a person from spirituality, the *yetzer hara* is preventing him from developing the very traits that are unique to humans, and is trying to reduce him to the level of a *beheimah* (animal). In *Tanya*, Rabbi Shneur Zalman quotes the Talmudic statement that a beast would not dare attack a person who bears the Divine image, for the Torah states, "I will make all beasts and animals fear you and tremble before you" (*Genesis* 9:2), and he says that the reason Daniel was not harmed by the lions was because he indeed bore "the image of G–d" in which man was created. To achieve this lofty status, we must do our utmost to develop ourselves to the highest level of spirituality within our capacity, for only then will we achieve "being like unto G–d." This leads us to the third deterrent from spirituality.

The *yetzer hara* may deprive a person of his feeling of dignity. In many of my writings I stress the importance of a healthy sense of self-esteem. A person should recognize his uniqueness as a human being and resist doing anything which would compromise his dignity and lower him to a subhuman level in even the slightest degree.

It is not beyond the wiles of the *yetzer hara* to masquerade as a friendly "spiritual" guide. It may mislead a person into thinking that the humility which is so central to spirituality requires that a person think of himself as worthless. It may exaggerate a person's defects as if to say, "There is no point in your aiming for spirituality. You are too far gone to become spiritual. You have sinned so grievously that you are beyond redemption. Why exert yourself in something which is futile? You can never amount to anything." The *yetzer hara* may try to convince a person that these feelings constitute *anivus* (humility), and that to feel dignified is nothing but *ga'avah* (vanity), which the Torah so soundly condemns.

It is not *ga'avah* to be aware of one's capacities, talents, and strengths. The noted ethicist, Rabbi Yehudah Leib Chasman, says that a person who does not know his strengths is not an *anav* (humble), but rather a fool. A person must know his capacity for greatness and seek to fulfill it by using the talents with which G–d has endowed him. No one, under any circumstances, should ever despair of being able to achieve the highest level of spirituality.

Temptation and delusion are thus the two primary weapons of the *yetzer hara*. In *Path of the Just,* RaMCHaL points out the specific ways in which the *yetzer hara* tries to deter a person from developing each spiritual trait; in order to avoid its seduction, we must be aware of these.

How does one resist the wiles of the *yetzer hara?* The Baal Shem Tov teaches us how to do this with an excellent parable, which we have mentioned previously.

A *king wished to test the loyalty of his subjects, and engaged a shrewd person to mix among the populace and foment rebellion. The agent did as he was told, telling people that the king was too oppressive and unjust, and that they would fare much better if they freed themselves from his rule. The weaker among them fell prey to this incitement and began to defy the king's orders. Those who were loyal to the king argued with the agent and attempted to disprove his points. The wisest among them reasoned that it was simply absurd to think that so powerful a king would allow someone to wander about freely fomenting rebellion. They understood that this could only be the king's way of testing their loyalty. They therefore said to the agent, "Look, we know exactly who you are and what you are up to. We know that it was the king that put you up to this, and you may go back to the king and report that you did your utmost, but that we were not even interested in arguing with you. You have done your duty, so don't bother us any more, and we will do ours."*

This is the ideal attitude toward the *yetzer hara*, which is only fulfilling its mission to test us. We should recognize this, and simply tell it that we understand what it is trying to do, but that we are loyal subjects of G–d and are not the least bit interested in what it has to say nor in getting into any arguments with it. Of course, the *yetzer hara* persists in its mission and repeatedly comes back, but our attitude should be to brush it off and simply say, "Get lost!"

The works on Torah ethics have many valuable suggestions on methods to resist the *yetzer hara*. If we implement them, we can have a powerful motivation for spirituality, comprised of both our innate desire for a closeness with G–d and our grasp of what it means to be created in His image.

41

Guides to Spirituality

Developing spirituality may, at the first glance, appear to be a difficult task, but in fact this is not so. In his parting words to the Israelites, Moses said, "It (the Torah) is not distant from you ... but is very close to you, in your mouth and in your heart to do it" (*Deuteronomy* 30:14). Lest one might argue that it is far from being close and is rather a formidable task, Moses immediately explains, "that which I instruct you to do *this day*" (ibid. 30:16); i.e., all one must undertake is the challenge of only the present day, not the future, not even tomorrow. Living spiritually today is not difficult, and inasmuch as there is nothing I can do today about tomorrow's challenge, there is no reason for me to be concerned now about tomorrow. If we look carefully at the covenant Moses contracted between G–d and Israel, we will see that he repeatedly refers to "this day" (*Deuteronomy* 29:9-30:20), because it is only by taking one day at a time that we can live spiritually.

Even so, however, we must have a clear concept of what spirituality is all about in order to attain it, and what methods we should use in its pursuit. In the past pages I have tried to describe the various traits that are essential to spirituality. Much of my material is taken from Torah works of ethics, and I strongly urge the study of these works. Among them are:

> *The Book of Proverbs*
> *Ethics of the Fathers*
> *The Letter of the Ramban*
> *Path of the Just (Mesillas Yesharim)*
> *Ways of the Righteous (Orchos Tzaddikim)*
> *Michtav MeEliyahu*

There are, of course, many other fine texts on *middos,* some of which are available in English.

Learning about spirituality is not a course which one completes in a single semester. RaMCHaL states in his introduction to *Path of the Just* that people are quite familiar with most of the principles of spirituality, but that strangely enough, precisely because they are so well known, people tend to take them for granted and not give them much consideration. He therefore recommends *repeatedly* reading *Path of the Just,* because this will emphasize what we already know.

Ramban also stresses the importance of frequently reviewing the components of spirituality. In his famous letter to his son, Ramban call his attention to several salient features of spirituality:

controlling expressions of anger
humility
giving thought before speaking
studying Torah
implementing what one has just learned

Ramban then goes on to instruct his son to read the letter *at least once a week*. Obviously, after reading the letter several times one would know its contents. But as RaMCHaL said, knowledge of spirituality is not enough. Too often such knowledge remains academic, and one must repeatedly be reminded to apply it.

The *yetzer hara* never relaxes its efforts to divert us from spirituality, and we must counter its manipulations by constantly reviewing the principles of spirituality.

An important guide to spirituality is emulating the behavior of highly spiritual people. Nothing is as impressive as personally seeing spirituality in action, and next best is hearing or reading about how our great Torah personalities implemented spirituality in their lives. We are fortunate in having biographies of a number of our *tzaddikim*, some of which were and are our contemporaries. There is also a rich repository of spirituality in anecdotes of the lives of *tzaddikim* of past generations. I have tried to make some of these available in *Not Just Stories* (*Shaar Press*, 1997).

But as important as reading is, it cannot in itself lead

to spirituality. One may read many articles about medicine, yet one consults a physician when a health problem arises, and does not treat oneself on the basis of the knowledge derived from reading. Rambam refers to Torah scholars as the "physicians of the soul" (*Eight Chapters*), and we should consult them about our spiritual defects. The principle "Make for yourself a teacher" (*Ethics of the Fathers* 1:6) is essential for achieving spirituality.

As we noted earlier, every person makes judgments about what to do and how to do it, and we must realize that our judgment capacities may be impaired by our personal interests and biases. It is therefore important that we check out our judgments with someone who can be more objective, and for this reason we are instructed: "Acquire for yourself a friend" (ibid.) The chassidic master, Rabbi Elimelech of Lizhensk, recommends that at the end of each day, we bare our souls to a trusted friend, relating all that we did and even thought that day. Airing one's thoughts and feelings and having someone more objective evaluate them can help us discover any faulty judgments we made. Again, the fact that Rabbi Elimelech instructs us to so *every day* underscores the point we made earlier, that the development of spirituality should be taken one day at a time.

Finally, we must pray fervently for Divine assistance in becoming spiritual. We have been assured that G–d will help us if we make a sincere effort at becoming spiritual. "Give Me an opening no greater than the point of a needle, and I will expand it to the size of the portals of a banquet hall" (*Shir HaShirim Rabbah* 5:3). However, our prayer must be accompanied by effort on our part. G–d will not do it for us if we sit back and do nothing.

> The Chafetz Chaim told a parable of a man who approached a wealthy person and asked for a loan so that he could open a business. "Very well," the rich man said. "Come to my home tonight and I will give you the money."
>
> The following day the man again asked him for a loan. "I waited for you last night to give you the money, but you never came. Come to my home tonight and you can have it."
>
> The man did not come the second night either, and the next morning he again asked for a loan. "What is it with you?" the rich man asked. "If you want the money, why don't you come for it? And if you don't want it, why are you repeatedly asking for it?"

So it is with us, said the Chafetz Chaim. We pray that G–d enlighten us with the wisdom of the Torah, but we do not come to the *beis midrash* to receive it. If we do not make the effort to study Torah, learn about spirituality, and begin to act spiritually, we can hardly pray for Divine assistance. G–d will give it to us, but we must come for it.

If we have a cheap appliance, we may try to operate it by trial and error. But if it we have a very expensive appliance and improper operation can damage it, we read the directions very carefully. If we truly value our spiritual lives, we should act accordingly.

Epilogue

eloved is man, for he was created in G–d's image; it is indicative of a greater love that it was made known to him that he was created in G–d's image. Beloved are the people Israel for a cherished utensil (Torah) was given to them; it is indicative of a greater love that it was made known to them that they were given a cherished utensil" (*Ethics of the Fathers* 3:18).

These are the two essential elements of spirituality: for a person to know (1) that he was created in the Divine image and (2) that he was given the instructions and guidelines for developing the Divine component of his being.

G–d did not bring the world into being in order that there would be mountains and rivers, giraffes and alligators. The universe was created so that there would be man, who would bring the Divine presence into the physical world. All that preceded creation of man was preparatory, and the actual beginning of the world was therefore the creation of man.

In *Ecclesiastes,* Solomon proposes various ideas to which a person is vulnerable: that there is no qualitative difference between man and animal (3:19); that we might as well seek to maximize all physical gratifications (9:7); that the wise man and the fool share a common fate (9:2). At the close of *Ecclesiastes,* Solomon rejects all these ideas by saying, "In summation, after all has been considered, one should revere G–d and obey His mitzvos, for that is the essence of man" (12:13).

In the past chapters I have essentially tried to elaborate on this verse, and to show in which ways a person can and should develop his uniquely human capacities. Man was made aware of his potential for Divinity, commissioned to develop this potential, and given the instructions as to how he can achieve this. Solomon sums it up simply and succinctly: to revere G–d and observe His mitzvos.

Reverence of G–d includes emulating His attributes, and the fulfillment of mitzvos includes the development of proper *middos* in addition to performing the various rituals. When we do so, we acknowledge the "Divine image" in other people and treat them accordingly, and because we appreciate our own Divine image, we behave in a manner which benefits us.

Some people may think that there are other ways of achieving the spirituality which is man's uniqueness. Solomon's statement is clear: After *everything* has been considered, all possible positions, there is only one way to achieve the essence of man: to revere G–d and follow His mitzvos. Any other formula for spirituality is spurious.

The book of *Ecclesiastes* is read on the festival of

Succos, the season of rejoicing, when the completion of the harvest provides a person with the means for gratifying one's mundane aspirations. It is at this time that we are reminded of Solomon's analysis of life and his final conclusion.

When our culture was primarily agricultural, it sufficed to hear the message of *Ecclesiastes* on Succos. In modern times, the miracles of science and technology have so enriched our lives with mundane gratifications that we need to repeatedly review Solomon's conclusion.

Many young people who have grown up lacking for nothing in a material sense have been disillusioned with the pursuit of pleasure as the goal in life. Some have fled to the Oriental religions in search of meaning, whereas others have capitulated to the pursuit of pleasure, and finding it grossly inadequate, have fled into the oblivion and euphoria of drugs. The person who sincerely devotes himself to a comprehensive Torah lifestyle need not look elsewhere. His life takes on meaning as he pursues not the pleasures of life, but the happiness of fulfilling himself as the "*mentsch*" that G–d intended him to be: *spiritual man.*

It is my hope that the teachings of our Torah personalities, both in their works and in their actions, help us achieve the true happiness which dignifies the human being: the striving for spiritual perfection.

This, then, is the essence of Jewish spirituality: to rise above one's physical self, to be truly free in determining one's behavior and goals in life, and to implement the teachings of Torah.